studysync®

Reading & Writing Companion

Trying Times

Who are you in a crisis?

:: studysync®

studysync.com

Send all inquiries to:
BookheadEd Learning, LLC
610 Daniel Young Drive
Sonoma, CA 95476

ISBN 978-1-94-469589-7

7 8 9 10 11 12 LMN 26 25 24 23 22

C

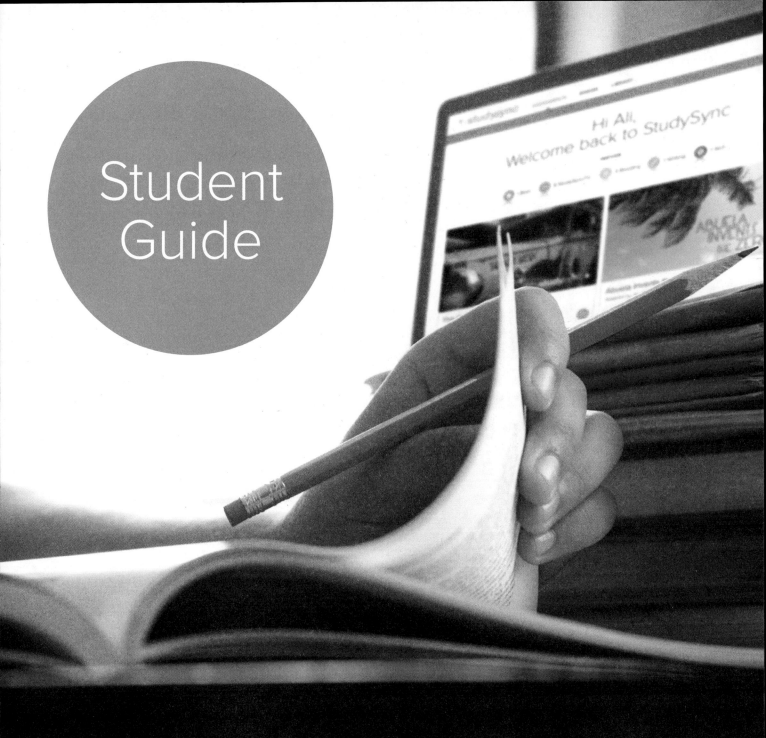

Student
Guide

Getting Started

Welcome to the StudySync Reading & Writing Companion! In this book, you will find a collection of readings based on the theme of the unit you are studying. As you work through the readings, you will be asked to answer questions and perform a variety of tasks designed to help you closely analyze and understand each text selection. Read on for an explanation of each section of this book.

Close Reading and Writing Routine

In each unit, you will read texts that share a common theme, despite their different genres, time periods, and authors. Each reading encourages a closer look through questions and a short writing assignment.

1 Introduction

An Introduction to each text provides historical context for your reading as well as information about the author. You will also learn about the genre of the text and the year in which it was written.

2 Notes

Many times, while working through the activities after each text, you will be asked to **annotate** or **make annotations** about what you are reading. This means that you should highlight or underline words in the text and use the "Notes" column to make comments or jot down any questions you have. You may also want to note any unfamiliar vocabulary words here.

You will also see sample student annotations to go along with the Skill lesson for that text.

③ First Read

During your first reading of each selection, you should just try to get a general idea of the content and message of the reading. Don't worry if there are parts you don't understand or words that are unfamiliar to you. You'll have an opportunity later to dive deeper into the text.

④ Think Questions

These questions will ask you to start thinking critically about the text, asking specific questions about its purpose, and making connections to your prior knowledge and reading experiences. To answer these questions, you should go back to the text and draw upon specific evidence to support your responses. You will also begin to explore some of the more challenging vocabulary words in the selection.

⑤ Skills

Each Skill includes two parts: Checklist and Your Turn. In the Checklist, you will learn the process for analyzing the text. The model student annotations in the text provide examples of how you might make your own notes following the instructions in the Checklist. In the Your Turn, you will use those same instructions to practice the skill.

---

③  First Read

Read "The Tell-Tale Heart." After you read, complete the Think Questions below.

④ **THINK QUESTIONS**

1. Write two or three sentences explaining how the narrator feels about the old man and why he decides to murder him.

2. Does the narrator seem trustworthy as he gives his account of the events in the story? Cite evidence from the text to explain your opinions.

3. What sound does the narrator hear at the end of the story that causes him to confess to the murder? Provide evidence to support your inference.

4. Find the word **sufficient** in paragraph 3 of "The Tell-Tale Heart." Use context clues in the surrounding sentences, as well as the sentence in which the word appears, to determine the word's meaning. Write your definition here and identify clues that helped you figure out its meaning.

5. Use context clues to determine the meaning of **sagacity** as it is used in paragraph 4 of "The Tell-Tale Heart." Write your definition here and identify clues that helped you figure out its meaning. Then check the meaning in a dictionary.

---

⑤ **LANGUAGE, STYLE, AND AUDIENCE** Skill: Language, Style, and Audience

Use the Checklist to analyze Language, Style, and Audience in "The Tell-Tale Heart." Refer to the sample student annotations about Language, Style, and Audience in the text.

••• CHECKLIST FOR LANGUAGE, STYLE, AND AUDIENCE

In order to determine an author's style, do the following:

✓ identify and define any unfamiliar words or phrases

✓ use context, including the meanings of surrounding words and phrases

✓ note possible reactions to the author's word choice

✓ examine your reaction to the author's word choice

✓ identify any analogies, or comparisons in which one part of the comparison helps explain the other

To analyze the impact of specific word choice on meaning and tone, ask the following questions:

✓ How did your understanding of the language change during your analysis?

✓ How do the writer's word choices impact or create meaning in the text?

✓ How do the writer's word choices impact or create a specific tone in the text?

✓ How could various audiences interpret this language? What different possible emotional responses can you list?

✓ What analogies do you see? Where might an analogy have clarified meaning or created a specific tone?

---

⑤ **↻ YOUR TURN**

1. What effect do the punctuation choices in paragraphs 9 and 10 have on the tone?

   ○ A. The dashes and exclamation marks reveal that the narrator is losing control.
   ○ B. The italics make it clear that the narrator's words aren't to be trusted.
   ○ C. The semicolons introduce a formal tone into an informal speech.
   ○ D. The frequent questions reveal the narrator's attempt to engage the reader.

2. Which phrase from the passage most clearly suggests the narrator's disturbed mental state at the end of the story?

   ○ A. "but I talked more fluently"
   ○ B. "Why would they not be gone?"
   ○ C. "It grew louder—louder—louder!"
   ○ D. "And still the men chatted pleasantly"

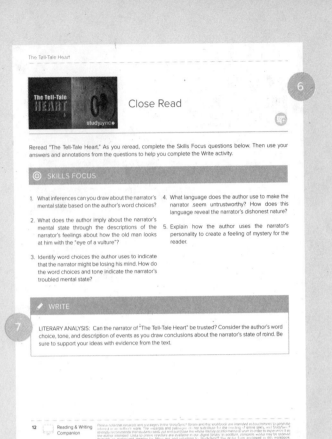

6 Close Read & Skills Focus

6 Close Read & Skills Focus

After you have completed the First Read, you will be asked to go back and read the text more closely and critically. Before you begin your Close Read, you should read through the Skills Focus to get an idea of the concepts you will want to focus on during your second reading. You should work through the Skills Focus by making annotations, highlighting important concepts, and writing notes or questions in the "Notes" column. Depending on instructions from your teacher, you may need to respond online or use a separate piece of paper to start expanding on your thoughts and ideas.

7 Write

Your study of each selection will end with a writing assignment. For this assignment, you should use your notes, annotations, personal ideas, and answers to both the Think and Skills Focus Questions. Be sure to read the prompt carefully and address each part of it in your writing.

8 English Language Learner

The English Language Learner texts focus on improving language proficiency. You will practice learning strategies and skills in individual and group activities to become better readers, writers, and speakers.

 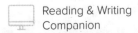

Extended Writing Project and Grammar

This is your opportunity to use genre characteristics and craft to compose meaningful, longer written works exploring the theme of each unit. You will draw information from your readings, research, and own life experiences to complete the assignment.

1 Writing Project

After you have read all of the unit text selections, you will move on to a writing project. Each project will guide you through the process of writing your essay. Student models will provide guidance and help you organize your thoughts. One unit ends with an **Extended Oral Project** which will give you an opportunity to develop your oral language and communication skills.

2 Writing Process Steps

There are four steps in the writing process: Plan, Draft, Revise, and Edit and Publish. During each step, you will form and shape your writing project, and each lesson's peer review will give you the chance to receive feedback from your peers and teacher.

3 Writing Skills

Each Skill lesson focuses on a specific strategy or technique that you will use during your writing project. Each lesson presents a process for applying the skill to your own work and gives you the opportunity to practice it to improve your writing.

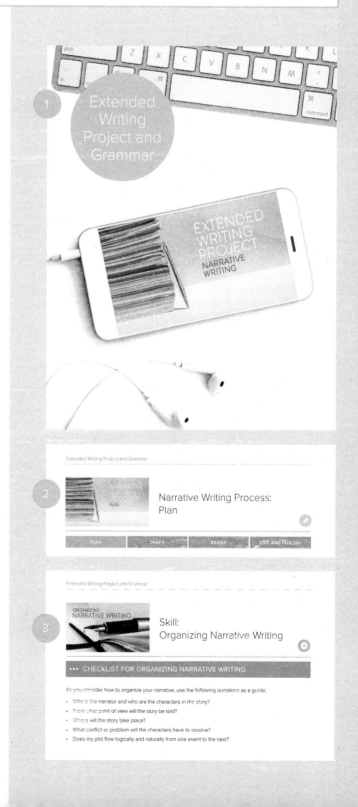

1 Extended Writing Project and Grammar

EXTENDED WRITING PROJECT
NARRATIVE WRITING

Extended Writing Project and Grammar

2 Narrative Writing Process: Plan

| PLAN | DRAFT | REVISE | EDIT AND PUBLISH |

Extended Writing Project and Grammar

3 Skill: Organizing Narrative Writing

••• CHECKLIST FOR ORGANIZING NARRATIVE WRITING

As you consider how to organize your narrative, use the following questions as a guide:

- Who is the narrator and who are the characters in the story?
- From what point of view will the story be told?
- Where will the story take place?
- What conflict or problem will the characters have to resolve?
- Does my plot flow logically and naturally from one event to the next?

Trying Times

Who are you in a crisis?

Genre Focus: DRAMA

Texts

 Paired Readings

Please note that excerpts and passages in the StudySync® library and this workbook are intended as touchstones to generate interest in an author's work. The excerpts and passages do not substitute for the reading of entire texts, and StudySync® strongly recommends that students seek out and purchase the whole literary or informational work in order to experience it as the author intended. Links to online resellers are available in our digital library. In addition, complete works may be ordered through an authorized reseller by filling out and returning to StudySync® the order form enclosed in this workbook.

Extended Oral Project and Grammar

English Language Learner Resources

Please note that excerpts and passages in the StudySync® library and this workbook are intended as touchstones to generate interest in an author's work. The excerpts and passages do not substitute for the reading of entire texts, and StudySync® strongly recommends that students seek out and purchase the whole literary or informational work in order to experience it as the author intended. Links to online resellers are available in our digital library. In addition, complete works may be ordered through an authorized reseller by filling out and returning to StudySync® the order form enclosed in this workbook.

Unit 5: Trying Times
Who are you in a crisis?

WINSTON CHURCHILL

Winston Churchill (1874–1965) was appointed Prime Minister of Britain just months after the outbreak of World War II. In the first of many morale-boosting speeches he delivered to inspire the British to keep fighting against the seemingly invincible enemy that was Nazi Germany, he famously borrowed the words of Theodore Roosevelt when he said, "I have nothing to offer but blood, toil, tears, and sweat." Churchill helped shape the Allied strategy during the war and is credited with leading his country to victory from the brink of defeat.

ANNE FRANK

Born in the German city of Frankfurt am Main, Anne Frank (1929–1945) moved with her family to Amsterdam when anti-Semitism started to increase in prevalence with the rise of Nazi Germany. As the situation continued to escalate, Frank's father furnished a secret annex at his place of work. During the two years that the family spent in hiding there, Anne kept a journal tracking her thoughts and feelings about the events taking place. Her journal ends abruptly when her family is captured and deported.

FRANCES GOODRICH AND ALBERT HACKETT

Frances Goodrich (1890–1984) and Albert Hackett (1900–1995) were a Hollywood screenwriting duo who wrote more than thirty popular screenplays. Their adaptation of *Anne Frank's The Diary of a Young Girl* debuted in 1955 as *The Diary of Anne Frank: A Play*. The play situated Frank's personal account of her wartime experiences within a broader historical context, and, as *New York Times* drama critic Brooks Atkinson wrote, "let a clean, young mind address the conscience of the world."

JEANNE WAKATSUKI HOUSTON AND JAMES D. HOUSTON

Not long after Japan bombed the US naval base at Pearl Harbor in 1941, the FBI sent California residents Jeanne Wakatsuki Houston (b. 1934) and her family to the Manzanar internment camp. Only seven years old at the time, Wakatsuki Houston was one of more than 10,000 Japanese Americans that had been imprisoned by the time Japan surrendered in 1945. In her memoir, *Farewell to Manzanar* (1973), which she wrote with her husband James D. Houston, she recalls the feelings of sadness, confusion, and incredulity that she experienced during her time there.

NELSON MANDELA

In 1962, Nelson Mandela (1918–2013) was sentenced to life in prison for his role in opposing South Africa's system of apartheid, or enforced segregation. His reputation grew steadily while he was in prison and he gained international support. He was released from captivity in 1990 and became South Africa's first democratically-elected president in 1994. A large portion of his autobiography *Long Walk to Freedom* (1994) details his experience in prison, which he portrays as a microcosm of the apartheid world.

CLAUDE MCKAY

Although he started out writing about peasant life in rural Jamaica, Claude McKay (1889–1948) is best known for his fiction and poetry addressing racial injustice in the United States. Regarded as a key figure in the Harlem Renaissance, McKay started getting involved in social causes when he moved to the United States in the 1920s. Much of his poetry is about the importance of standing one's ground in the face of hardship. In "If We Must Die," he describes being "Pressed to the wall, dying, but fighting back!"

ELIE WIESEL

Romanian-born writer, lecturer, and humanities professor Elie Wiesel (1928–2016) was fifteen years old when he and his family were sent to the Nazi concentration camp Auschwitz. After the war, he became a spokesperson for Holocaust survivors and published a memoir, *Night* (1958), describing his horrific experiences. He lectured frequently on global humanitarian issues to raise awareness of groups persecuted for religion, race, or national origin. When he was awarded the Nobel Peace Prize in 1986, the committee called him a "messenger to mankind."

ELEANOR AYER

Eleanor Ayer (b. 1947) has written many young adult nonfiction books, many of which are about the Holocaust. Her dual biography, *Parallel Journeys* (1995), chronicles the events of World War II through the lives of Helen Waterford, a Jewish woman who survived Auschwitz, and Alfons Heck, a German member of the Hitler Youth organization. The book excerpts passages from Waterford's and Heck's individual memoirs, which Ayer had previously edited. This unlikely duo gave speeches on the horrors of the war and on what it would take to heal its wounds.

EKNATH EASWARAN

Spiritual teacher, author, and translator of Indian religious texts, Eknath Easwaran (1910–1999) wrote over forty books on meditation and world mysticism in his lifetime. Born in southern India, his spirituality was shaped at an early age by his close relationship with his grandmother. After his grandmother died, a visit to Mahatma Gandhi's ashram inspired him to turn to meditation to cope with his loss. An interest in English literature took him to Northern California where he founded the Blue Mountain Center of Meditation in 1961.

ALAN GRATZ

North Carolina–based writer Alan Gratz (b. 1972) has published numerous young adult fiction and fantasy novels, including his popular alternate history novel, *Samurai Shortstop* (2006). His 2017 book *Refugee* tells the stories of three kids: a Jewish boy in Nazi Germany in the 1930s, a Cuban girl in 1994, and a Syrian boy in 2015, tied together by their common struggle to escape persecution and find refuge.

LUCY WANG

Chinese American playwright and performer Lucy Wang grew up in Akron, Ohio, and now lives in Los Angeles. Wang has written numerous plays on subjects as varied as Asian American identity, family dynamics, and climate change. In her 2012 comedy *Teen Mogul,* a young girl's life is upended when her mother leaves their family. Instead of wallowing in despair, she decides to pursue a pipe dream and contact her favorite mogul for a job that would restore her family's stability.

Teen Mogul

DRAMA
Lucy Wang
2012

Introduction

Her first career having begun in New York City's high financial world, Lucy Wang was uniquely qualified to write her acclaimed first play, *Junk Bonds*, which earned her a Lucy Award from the Kennedy Center and set her new career as a playwright on the fast track. *Teen Mogul*, featured here, also builds off of Wang's roots in business. When 15-year-old protagonist Tracy's mother abandons the family, leaving them in emotional and financial tumult, Tracy takes matters into her own hands by landing a high-paying gig as a marketing director. In this scene—inspired by 12-year-old Steve Jobs calling a Hewlett-Packard co-founder and landing a job—Tracy pitches herself at a lunch meeting with the mogul Christopher Brennan.

"Well, don't keep a mogul waiting, let's see what you got."

NOTES

SCENE 7

1   *(Diner. Tracy eats voraciously during her job interview with CHRISTOPHER BRENNAN)*

2   CHRISTOPHER: Wow, you sure can eat. I've never seen a woman eat with such wild abandon. And you look like you're enjoying the food too. You're not just bingeing.

3   TRACY: Oh, I guess I should have eaten breakfast *(Puts her fork down:)* But I hate breakfast. I find the choices too limiting.

4   CHRISTOPHER: I can see why. Cheeseburger. Fries. Clam Chowder. Salad. Unsweetened ice tea. Not exactly breakfast foods. You know, early in my career, I had to decide, do I gnaw on the chicken bone, or do I want that job?

5   TRACY: Sorry. I just assumed we'd talk about the job after we ate.

6   CHRISTOPHER: Don't apologize. I love a woman with a **voracious** appetite.

7   TRACY: You do?

8   CHRISTOPHER: I hate it when I take my date out to a five star restaurant and all she wants is a tiny garden salad. Makes me furious.

9   TRACY: Oh I'd never do that.

10 CHRISTOPHER: I don't suppose it's in your DNA.

11 TRACY: Not yet. Maybe I'll mutate when I'm older. I'm told it happens.

12 CHRISTOPHER: People with voracious appetites make the best employees. They're hungry. And if they eat in front of you, you know they're honest. As

Please note that excerpts and passages in the StudySync® library and this workbook are intended as touchstones to generate interest in an author's work. The excerpts and passages do not substitute for the reading of entire texts, and StudySync® strongly recommends that students seek out and purchase the whole literary or informational work in order to experience it as the author intended. Links to online resellers are available in our digital library. In addition, complete works may be ordered through an authorized reseller by filling out and returning to StudySync® the order form enclosed in this workbook.

Reading & Writing Companion   1

opposed to those critters who eat a salad in front of you and when you're not looking, raid the entire refrigerator.

13   TRACY: Well, in that case, don't mind if I take another big, delicious bite.

14   CHRISTOPHER: You must work out. To eat like a teenager.

15   TRACY: Oh. Yes. I have very high metabolism. Plus I ride my bike everywhere.

16   CHRISTOPHER: Hard-core environmentalist.

17   TRACY: Could be, someday.

18   CHRISTOPHER: So, I looked over your resume. Very impressive.

19   TRACY: Thank you.

20   CHRISTOPHER: Watching you eat, however, makes me wonder why did you fold your Chinese dumpling business? Seems to me, food is your passion.

21   TRACY: Food is so labor intensive. Not that I'm afraid of work. I'm not. But I was tired of smelling of dough, egg-wash, ginger and soy sauce 24/7.

22   CHRISTOPHER: Sounds **sublime** to me. Cleveland is not known for its winning Chinese cuisine.

23   TRACY: Believe me, I know. My father's number one complaint.

24   CHRISTOPHER: The other thing is, did you go to college?

25   TRACY: Steve Jobs, Michael Dell, Bill Gates, they all dropped out.

26   CHRISTOPHER: So you're a college dropout.

27   TRACY: No. Not exactly. I did take a math class at Kent State once. I want to study more, but my father, he's not well, and . . . *(Tracy starts to tremble, voice falters)*

28   CHRISTOPHER: I'm so sorry.

29   TRACY: Me too, me too. It's **imperative** I step up and sacrifice.

30   CHRISTOPHER: Yes, it all makes sense now.

31   TRACY: I still want to. Some day. But not everyone needs to graduate from college to be successful, right? Look at you. You dropped out of Stanford.

Reading & Writing Companion

32 CHRISTOPHER: You've done your homework.

33 TRACY: I excel at homework. Homework is my favorite subject.

34 CHRISTOPHER: So why do you want to work for me?

35 TRACY: Like me, you have something to prove. And I can get you there.

36 CHRISTOPHER: This sounds very interesting.

37 TRACY: Every time you start something new, it turns to gold. But then your investors[1], your shareholders[2] they all say your management style sucks. You're too **mercurial**, unable to trust and delegate, you shoot your best people down, causing a divide as vast as the Grand Canyon.

38 CHRISTOPHER: Harsh.

39 TRACY: Sensing a lucrative opportunity, corporate raiders like Duke Manning swoop in and hostile take-over. You're through. Ejected. Bird doo.

40 CHRISTOPHER: Anyone ever tell you maybe you should get out there more, live a little, and screw homework?

41 TRACY: Uh, no.

42 CHRISTOPHER: And why should I trust you who comes forth with slings and arrows?

43 TRACY: I'm going to share some of my new ideas with you, and I'm going to offer to work for you for two weeks free. If you don't like what I do, no obligation. But if you do like what I have to offer, you make me an offer I can't refuse. Deal?

44 CHRISTOPHER: Let me see some of these new ideas you have.

45 *(Tracy pulls out her computer bag. It's not her computer. It's Kevin's computer and stuff.)*

46 TRACY: Oh my god. This computer. It's not—

47 CHRISTOPHER: What's wrong?

Skill: Dramatic Elements and Structure

Tracy has done her homework and knows a lot about Christopher's company. Here she is during the interview, trying to impress him, but then she tells Christopher his "management style sucks." Next she says he might be ejected from his company and become "bird doo"! The style here is abrupt and funny.

---

1. **investor** person who put money into a business venture with the expectation of receiving a profit
2. **shareholder** owner of the financial stakes of a company

NOTES

Skill:
Plot

The incident with Kevin and the computer bag mix-up proves to Christopher that these bags really do look alike. This happens before Tracy shows him anything on her computer. It reveals just how clever Tracy is.

48 *(Kevin races over. He snuck in earlier and hid.)*

49 KEVIN: Miss, I believe this is yours.

50 TRACY: *(Relieved:)* Of course. We must have switched at the . . . at the . . .

51 KEVIN: Bank. I followed you when I realized, I didn't want to interrupt, but–

52 TRACY: Thank you. I'm so sorry.

53 KEVIN: It's not your fault. They all look alike.

54 TRACY: They do, don't they?

55 KEVIN: Well, I better let you get back to whatever.

56 CHRISTOPHER: Yes. Please. This young woman promised to rock my world.

57 *(Kevin leaves.)*

58 TRACY: The first thing we need to make is computer bags. They shouldn't all look alike. Big, black, clunky. Every "geek" deserves some style.

59 CHRISTOPHER: Especially geeks. Was this a complete setup?

60 TRACY: *(Giggles:)* Let's see what happens when we go online and shop for computer bags. Same, same, same.

61 CHRISTOPHER: Brilliant.

62 TRACY: I also designed our new company logo.

63 CHRISTOPHER: You're kidding. Whatever possessed you to undertake this task?

64 TRACY: Did you know Carolyn Knight was a student at Portland State when she designed the Nike Swoosh? She was given 35 dollars and 500 shares of stock.

65 CHRISTOPHER: I supposed this means you'd like to also be paid in stock.

66 TRACY: Oh, could I?

67 CHRISTOPHER: Well, don't keep a mogul waiting, let's see what you got.

68 TRACY: Thought you'd never ask. Exhibit A.

69   (OVERHEAD PROJECTION of "ADVANCE, INC." in different logos, fonts, colors, styles, graphic designs.)

70   (ADVANCE   ADVANCE)
      (ADVANCE   ADVANCE)
      (ADVANCE   ADVANCE)
      (ADVANCE   ADVANCE)
      (ADVANCE   ADVANCE)
      (ADVANCE   ADVANCE)
      (ADVANCE   ADVANCE)

71   TRACY: Steve Jobs started out in calligraphy and changed the world. Think of what we can do. It's our turn.

72   CHRISTOPHER: Really. Such a go-getter. You said ideas plural.

73   TRACY: (Pulls out some Chinese silk fabrics with gold threads, blues, reds, yellows, gold silver:) Rub these against your face. Think about what it might be like to sleep on these luxurious silks that come in **vibrant** colors. With gold threads. Dragons and phoenixes. Flowers.

74   CHRISTOPHER: Luxury high-end bedding. Nice and soft. You're hired. When can you start?

75   TRACY: Tomorrow too soon?

76   CHRISTOPHER: Bright and early.

77   TRACY: Actually I need some flexibility.

78   CHRISTOPHER: There's always a catch. What are you, on parole?

79   TRACY: In the morning, I need to . . . need to . . .

80   CHRISTOPHER: Take care of your dad. I get it.

81   TRACY: I can always be there after twelve noon. But in the mornings, I need to telecommute.

82   CHRISTOPHER: Fine. How much do you want?

83   TRACY: As in money?

84   CHRISTOPHER: Don't waffle now. Bring on the "homework."

Skill:
Plot

Tracy tells Christopher that Steve Jobs didn't start out as a computer genius. They can change the world, too. Then she shows him some silk bedding and says, "rub these against your face." When Christopher does, Tracy is hired.

85 TRACY: A hundred grand? With performance-based stock options, and signing bonus of ten grand.

86 CHRISTOPHER: Signing bonus! You were going to give me two weeks free.

87 TRACY: But I just realized I already did so much homework. Pretty please?

88 CHRISTOPHER: Done. How's Director of Marketing Research sound?

89 TRACY: You won't regret this.

90 CHRISTOPHER: I better not. Or I'll sue for damages. Kidding. Or, not.

(End of Scene 7)

First Read

Read *Teen Mogul*. After you read, complete the Think Questions below.

☁ THINK QUESTIONS

1. Why does Christopher make a comment about gnawing on the chicken bone? Cite textual evidence from the selection to support your answer.

2. According to Christopher, what are the favorable and unfavorable styles of eating for employees? Use evidence from the text to support your inferences.

3. What does Steve Jobs's calligraphy have to do with Tracy's pitch? Be sure to refer to the text for support.

4. Find the word **sublime** in line 22 of *Teen Mogul*. Use context clues in the surrounding sentences, as well as the sentence in which the word appears, to determine the word's meaning. Write your definition here and identify clues that helped you figure out its meaning.

5. Use context clues to determine the meaning of **imperative** as it is used in line 29 of *Teen Mogul*. Write your definition here and identify clues that helped you figure out its meaning. Then check the meaning in a dictionary.

PLOT

Skill:
Plot

Use the Checklist to analyze Plot in *Teen Mogul*. Refer to the sample student annotations about Plot in the text.

••• CHECKLIST FOR PLOT

In order to determine and analyze plot, consider the following:

✓ note how the plot unfolds throughout the story or drama, beginning with the inciting incident

✓ look for ways in which the decisions or actions of the characters alter or advance the events of the plot

✓ notice how dialogue or incidents propel, or push, the events of the plot to move in a particular direction or provoke, or cause, a decision.

✓ note how dialogue and events reveal aspects of a character

✓ look for the turning point in the drama, which leads to a resolution of the conflict

To evaluate plot, consider the following questions:

✓ How does the plot unfold in the story?

✓ What do dialogue and incidents in the drama reveal about the characters?

✓ How do dialogue and dramatic incidents propel the events of the plot?

PLOT

Skill:
Plot

Reread lines 82–90 of *Teen Mogul*. Then, using the Checklist on the previous page, answer the multiple-choice questions below.

⟳ YOUR TURN

1. What decision does Christopher make as a result of the conversation in these lines of dialogue?

   ○ A. Whether or not he will sue Tracy for damages
   ○ B. What Tracy's salary will be when she goes to work for him
   ○ C. That he should not give Tracy performance-based stock options
   ○ D. That he should give Tracy homework so she can learn about his company

2. Which of the following statements from Tracy best provokes Christopher to make this decision?

   ○ A. "With performance-based stock options, and signing bonus of ten grand."
   ○ B. "You won't regret this."
   ○ C. "But I just realized I already did so much homework. Pretty please?"
   ○ D. "As in money?"

Skill:
Dramatic Elements and Structure

Use the Checklist to analyze Dramatic Elements and Structure in *Teen Mogul*. Refer to the sample student annotations about Dramatic Elements and Structure in the text.

••• CHECKLIST FOR DRAMATIC ELEMENTS AND STRUCTURE

In order to determine how to compare and contrast the structures of two or more dramatic texts, note the following:

- ✓ the form of the drama, such as comedy or tragedy

- ✓ the characters and setting(s) by act and scene

- ✓ whether or how the setting changes in each act and scene

- ✓ the overall structures in the scenes and how they connect to the scenes' meanings

- ✓ stage directions and how they are used

- ✓ the style the author uses, including rhyming, formal, or realistic language

- ✓ how the acts and scenes advance the plot

- ✓ ways the structure of both texts are similar and different

To compare and contrast the structures of two or more texts and analyze how the differing structure of each text contributes to its meaning and style, use the following questions:

- ✓ How does each author introduce the characters?

- ✓ How does the setting in each drama contribute to the meaning of the text?

- ✓ How does the text's structure in each drama contribute to its style and meaning? Is the style meant to be realistic?

- ✓ How does the author's use of language in each drama contribute to the text's meaning?

- ✓ How do structure and choice of language affect the overall meaning of each drama? How do they compare?

Reading & Writing Companion

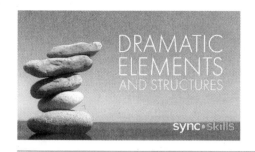

Skill:
Dramatic Elements and Structure

Reread lines 26–31 from *Teen Mogul* and read lines 25–27 of *The Diary of Anne Frank: A Play*. Then, using the Checklist on the previous page, answer the multiple-choice questions below.

⟳ YOUR TURN

1. Anne and Tracy are about the same age. How has trying to get an education affected both their lives?

   ○ A. Anne will continue to study after she goes into hiding, but Tracy must go to work.
   ○ B. Anne is going into hiding with her family, and Tracy is taking a math course at Kent State.
   ○ C. Anne is no longer able to go to a Dutch school and continue her education, and Tracy had to leave school but hopes to go back.
   ○ D. Tracy is upset that she cannot continue with her education, but Anne is not.

2. How does the voiceover of Anne and her father speaking together in this passage of *The Diary of Anne Frank: A Play* add a melancholy tone to the drama?

   ○ A. Mr. Frank's voice fades into Anne's voice, which signals a flashback as he recalls a painful memory.
   ○ B. It signals a flashback as Mr. Frank is going to tell Miep what happened in the attic.
   ○ C. The lights dim slowly to darkness, which creates a sad, melancholy tone to the play.
   ○ D. The voiceover reveals that Mr. Frank can't stay in Amsterdam

3. Why would using a voiceover from Tracy's father in *Teen Mogul* not be as effective as the voiceover in *The Diary of Anne Frank: A Play*?

   ○ A. Tracy's father is not aware that she is interviewing for a job with Christopher Brennan.
   ○ B. Tracy's father is ill, and the play is mostly about the funny relationship between Christopher and Tracy, so that would change the tone abruptly.
   ○ C. Tracy's father is too ill to do a voiceover.
   ○ D. Tracy's father would have nothing to add to the conversation between Tracy and Christopher.

Close Read

Reread *Teen Mogul*. As you reread, complete the Skills Focus questions below. Then use your answers and annotations from the questions to help you complete the Write activity.

SKILLS FOCUS

1. Identify one dramatic element in Scene 7 of *Teen Mogul,* such as character, setting, plot, dialogue, or stage directions, that reveal the play's comedic form.

2. Identify specific lines of dialogue or incidents in the play that help to propel the plot forward or provoke the characters to make certain decisions.

3. Analyze how specific lines of dialogue in *Teen Mogul* reveal aspects of Tracy's character and her motivations to get the job.

4. In *The Diary of Anne Frank: A Play,* the authors sometimes use stage directions to indicate how a character should say a particular line of dialogue. There are very few stage directions to indicate this in *Teen Mogul.* Why might an author use this method of structuring, or presenting, text in a drama, and why is it not necessary in *Teen Mogul*?

5. Describe how Tracy in *Teen Mogul* would answer the question, "Who are you in a crisis?" Use textual evidence to support your response.

WRITE

NARRATIVE: Write part of Scene 8 that continues the story of Tracy and Christopher Brennan. How might Tracy's attitude change when she reports for her first day of work? Will Christopher prove to be that "mercurial" boss that Tracy talked about during her interview? Think about dialogue or specific incidents you might include that continue and propel the action and keep the light, humorous tone of the play.

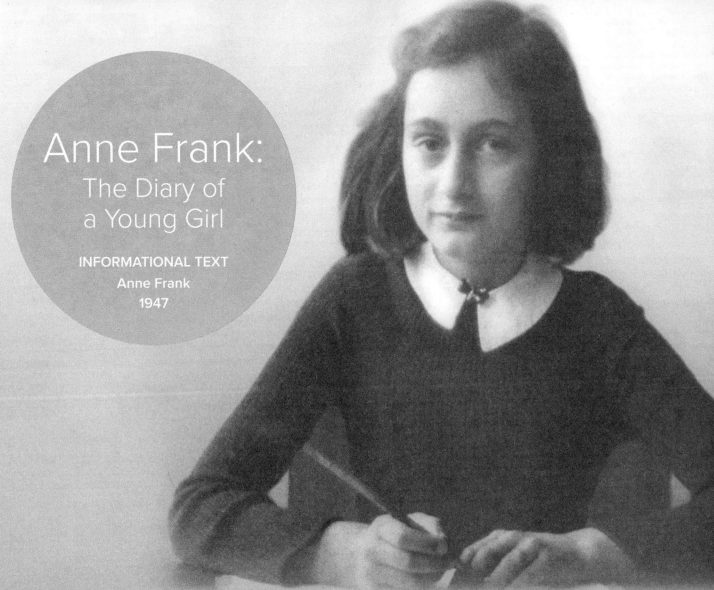

Anne Frank:
The Diary of a Young Girl

INFORMATIONAL TEXT
Anne Frank
1947

Introduction

studysync tv

From a secret annex, Anne Frank (1929–1945) kept a diary conveying the hopes and fears of an everyday teenager. But the times were anything but ordinary. Anne's diary begins two days after her 13th birthday and 22 days before she and her family are forced into hiding by the occupying Nazi army. Her diary ends abruptly more than two years later, when Anne and her family are captured and deported to Auschwitz. Anne died in a concentration camp just two weeks before it was liberated at the end of World War II; of those who were in hiding with her, only her father, Otto, survived. He took on the task of editing and publishing Anne's unique journal, a perspective of a young girl amidst the unimaginable horrors of the Holocaust. In the following excerpt, Anne's words portray her life both before and after being forced into hiding.

"So much has happened it's as if the whole world had suddenly turned upside down."

WEDNESDAY, JUNE 24, 1942

Dearest Kitty,

1   It's **sweltering.** Everyone is huffing and puffing, and in this heat I have to walk everywhere. Only now do I realize how pleasant a streetcar is, but we Jews are no longer allowed to make use of this luxury; our own two feet are good enough for us. Yesterday at lunchtime I had an appointment with the dentist on Jan Luykenstraat. It's a long way from our school on Stadstimmertuinen. That afternoon I nearly fell asleep at my desk. Fortunately, people automatically offer you something to drink. The dental assistant is really kind.

2   The only **mode** of transportation left to us is the ferry. The ferryman at Josef Israëlkade took us across when we asked him to. It's not the fault of the Dutch that we Jews are having such a bad time.

3   I wish I didn't have to go to school. My bike was stolen during Easter vacation, and Father gave Mother's bike to some Christian friends for safekeeping. Thank goodness summer vacation is almost here; one more week and our torment will be over.

4   Something unexpected happened yesterday morning. As I was passing the bicycle racks, I heard my name being called. I turned around and there was the nice boy I'd met the evening before at my friend Wilma's. He's Wilma's second cousin. I used to think Wilma was nice, which she is, but all she ever talks about is boys, and that gets to be a bore. He came toward me, somewhat shyly, and introduced himself as Hello Silberberg. I was a little surprised and wasn't sure what he wanted, but it didn't take me long to find out. He asked if I would allow him to **accompany** me to school. "As long as you're headed that way, I'll go with you," I said. And so we walked together. Hello is sixteen and good at telling all kinds of funny stories.

5   He was waiting for me again this morning, and I expect he will be from now on.

Anne

WEDNESDAY, JULY 8, 1942

Dearest Kitty,

6   It seems like years since Sunday morning. So much has happened it's as if the whole world had suddenly turned upside down. But as you can see, Kitty, I'm still alive, and that's the main thing, Father says. I'm alive all right, but don't ask where or how. You probably don't understand a word I'm saying today, so I'll begin by telling you what happened Sunday afternoon.

7   At three o'clock (Hello had left but was supposed to come back later), the doorbell rang. I didn't hear it, since I was out on the balcony, lazily reading in the sun. A little while later Margot appeared in the kitchen doorway looking very **agitated.** "Father has received a call-up notice from the SS[1]," she whispered. "Mother has gone to see Mr. van Daan." (Mr. van Daan is Father's business partner and a good friend.)

8   I was stunned. A call-up: everyone knows what that means. Visions of concentration camps and lonely cells raced through my head. How could we let Father go to such a fate? "Of course he's not going," declared Margot as we waited for Mother in the living room. "Mother's gone to Mr. van Daan to ask whether we can move to our hiding place tomorrow. The van Daans are going with us. There will be seven of us altogether." Silence. We couldn't speak. The thought of Father off visiting someone in the Jewish Hospital and completely unaware of what was happening, the long wait for Mother, the heat, the suspense — all this reduced us to silence.

9   Suddenly the doorbell rang again. "That's Hello," I said.

10 "Don't open the door!" exclaimed Margot to stop me. But it wasn't necessary, since we heard Mother and Mr. van Daan downstairs talking to Hello, and then the two of them came inside and shut the door behind them. Every time the bell rang, either Margot or I had to tiptoe downstairs to see if it was Father, and we didn't let anyone else in. Margot and I were sent from the room, as Mr. van Daan wanted to talk to Mother alone.

11 When she and I were sitting in our bedroom, Margot told me that the call-up was not for Father, but for her. At this second shock, I began to cry. Margot is

---

1. **the SS** a major paramilitary organization under Adolf Hitler and the Nazis, and later throughout German-occupied Europe during World War II, the SS was responsible for carrying out Nazi aggression and attacks

sixteen - apparently they want to send girls her age away on their own. But thank goodness she won't be going; Mother had said so herself, which must be what Father had meant when he talked to me about our going into hiding. Hiding . . . where would we hide? In the city? In the country? In a house? In a shack? When, where, how . . . ? These were questions I wasn't allowed to ask, but they still kept running through my mind.

12   Margot and I started packing our most important belongings into a schoolbag. The first thing I stuck in was this diary, and then curlers, handkerchiefs, schoolbooks, a comb and some old letters. Preoccupied by the thought of going into hiding, I stuck the craziest things in the bag, but I'm not sorry.

Yours, Anne

SATURDAY, JULY 11, 1942

Dearest Kitty,

13   Father, Mother, and Margot still can't get used to the chiming of the Westertoren clock, which tells us the time every quarter of an hour. Not me, I liked it from the start; it sounds so reassuring, especially at night. You no doubt want to hear what I think of being in hiding. Well, all I can say is that I don't really know yet. I don't think I'll ever feel at home in this house, but that doesn't mean I hate it. It's more like being on vacation in some strange pension[2]. Kind of an odd way to look at life in hiding, but that's how things are. The Annex is an ideal place to hide in. It may be damp and lopsided, but there's probably not a more comfortable hiding place in all of Amsterdam. No, in all of Holland.

14   Up to now our bedroom, with its blank walls, was very bare. Thanks to Father — who brought my entire postcard and movie-star collection here before hand — and to a brush and a pot of glue, I was able to plaster the wall with pictures. It looks much more cheerful. When the Van Daans arrive, we'll be able to build cupboards and other odds and ends out of the wood piled in the attic.

15   Margot and Mother have **recovered** somewhat. Yesterday Mother felt well enough to cook split-pea soup for the first time, but then she was downstairs talking and forgot all about it. The beans were scorched black, and no amount of scraping could get them out of the pan.

16   Last night the four of us went down to the private office and listened to England on the radio. I was so scared someone might hear it that I literally

---

2. **pension** a boarding house or small hotel in continental Europe which offers lodging and certain services

begged Father to take me back upstairs. Mother understood my **anxiety** and went with me. Whatever we do, we're very afraid the neighbors might hear or see us. . . .

Yours, Anne

Excerpted from *Anne Frank: The Diary of a Young Girl* by Anne Frank, published by Doubleday.

✏ WRITE

PERSONAL RESPONSE: What do you know about Anne Frank from this diary excerpt? What do you learn about her circumstances? Use textual evidence to explain any inferences. Finally, think about the use of a diary—Anne calls hers *Kitty*—to share this information. How might you use a diary? What makes a diary different from other kinds of communication?

Please note that excerpts and passages in the StudySync® library and this workbook are intended as touchstones to generate interest in an author's work. The excerpts and passages do not substitute for the reading of entire texts, and StudySync® strongly recommends that students seek out and purchase the whole literary or informational work in order to experience it as the author intended. Links to online resellers are available in our digital library. In addition, complete works may be ordered through an authorized reseller by filling out and returning to StudySync® the order form enclosed in this workbook.

Reading & Writing Companion   17

The Diary of Anne Frank: A Play

DRAMA
Frances Goodrich
and Albert Hackett
1955

Introduction

Frances Goodrich (1890–1984) and Albert Hackett (1900–1995) were married American screenwriters who created a play based on Anne Frank's *The Diary of a Young Girl*. It provides a dramatized account of the persecution of the Jewish people by the Nazis during World War II, offering another perspective on young Anne's tragic life as told through her diary. In this excerpt from the beginning of the play, the war is over, and Miep Gies, one of the family's confidants, has found the diary Anne kept during the war. After she presents it to Anne's bereaved father, Otto Frank, much of the play's action occurs in flashback, as Anne's diary transports Mr. Frank back to when the family lived in hiding and Anne was still alive.

"I've come to say good-bye . . .
I'm leaving here, Miep."

Act I, Scene 1

1 *The curtain rises on an empty stage. It is late afternoon November, 1945.*

2 *The rooms are dusty, the curtains in rags. Chairs and tables are overturned.*

3 *The door at the foot of the small stairwell swings open. MR. FRANK comes up the steps into view. He is a gentle, **cultured** European in his middle years. There is still a **trace** of a German accent in his speech.*

4 *He stands looking slowly around, making a supreme effort at self-control. He is weak, ill. His clothes are threadbare.*

5 *After a second he drops his rucksack on the couch and moves slowly about. He opens the door to one of the smaller rooms, and then **abruptly** closes it again, turning away. He goes to the window at the back, looking off at the Westertoren as its carillon[1] strikes the hour of six, then he moves restlessly on.*

6 *From the street below, we hear the sound of a barrel organ and children's voices at play. There is a many-colored scarf hanging from a nail. MR. FRANK takes it, putting it around his neck. As he starts back for his rucksack, his eye is caught by something lying on the floor. It is a woman's white glove. He holds it in his hand and suddenly all of his self-control is gone. He breaks down, crying.*

7 *We hear footsteps on the stairs. MIEP GIES comes up, looking for MR. FRANK. MIEP is a Dutch girl of about twenty-two. She wears a coat and hat, ready to go home. She is pregnant. Her **attitude** toward MR. FRANK is protective, compassionate.*

8 MIEP: Are you all right, Mr. Frank?

9 MR. FRANK *[quickly controlling himself]:* Yes, Miep, yes.

---

1. **carillon** a set of bells in a tower

Skill:
Word Meaning

When I look in a dictionary, I see that the third meaning of *supreme* fits the context of the sentence. It describes the kind of effort— intense, or great—that Mr. Frank was making to control his feelings. So I was right.

Copyright © BookheadEd Learning, LLC

NOTES

Skill: Dramatic
Elements and
Structure

*The setting is the same
apartment where the
Franks hid in
Amsterdam. Mr. Frank's
dialogue suggests he
has too many bad
memories of the place.
He comes across as a
sympathetic character,
a fine and caring man.
But he is also sad and
broken. He says that he
is bitter, but then asks
Miep's forgiveness.*

10   MIEP: Everyone in the office has gone home . . . It's after six. *[then pleading]* Don't stay up here, Mr. Frank. What's the use of torturing yourself like this?

11   MR. FRANK: I've come to say good-bye . . . I'm leaving here, Miep.

12   MIEP: What do you mean? Where are you going? Where?

13   MR. FRANK: I don't know yet. I haven't decided.

14   MIEP: Mr. Frank, you can't leave here! This is your home! Amsterdam is your home. Your business is here, waiting for you . . . You're needed here . . . Now that the war is over, there are things that . . .

15   MR. FRANK: I can't stay in Amsterdam, Miep. It has too many memories for me. Everywhere there's something . . . the house we lived in . . . the school . . . that street organ playing out there . . . I'm not the person you used to know, Miep. I'm a bitter old man. *[breaking off]* Forgive me, I shouldn't speak to you like this . . . after all that you did for us . . . the suffering . . .

16   MIEP: No. No. It wasn't suffering. You can't say we suffered. *[As she speaks, she straightens a chair which is overturned.]*

17   MR. FRANK: I know what you went through, you and Mr. Kraler. I'll remember it as long as I live. *[He gives one last look around.]* Come, Miep. *[He starts for the steps, then remembers his rucksack, going back to get it.]*

18   MIEP *[hurrying up to a cupboard]*: Mr. Frank, did you see? There are some of your papers here. *[She brings a bundle of papers to him.]* We found them in a heap of rubbish on the floor after . . . after you left.

19   MR. FRANK: Burn them. *[He opens his rucksack to put the glove in it.]*

20   MIEP: But, Mr. Frank, there are letters, notes . . .

21   MR. FRANK: Burn them. All of them.

22   MIEP: Burn *this?* *[She hands him a paperbound notebook.]*

23   MR FRANK *[quietly]*: Anne's diary. *[He opens the diary and begins to read.]* "Monday, the sixth of July, nineteen forty-two." *[to MIEP]* Nineteen forty-two. Is it possible, Miep? . . . Only three years ago. *[As he continues his reading, he sits down on the couch.]* "Dear Diary, since you and I are going to be great friends, I will start by telling you about myself. My name is Anne Frank. I am thirteen years old. I was born in Germany the twelfth of June, nineteen twenty-nine. As my family is Jewish, we emigrated to Holland when Hitler came to power."

NOTES

24 [As MR. FRANK *reads, another voice joins his, as if coming from the air. It is* ANNE'S VOICE.]

25 MR. FRANK and ANNE: "My father started a business, importing spice and herbs. Things went well for us until nineteen forty. Then the war came, and the Dutch capitulation, followed by the arrival of the Germans. Then things got very bad for the Jews."

26 [MR. FRANK'S VOICE *dies out.* ANNE'S VOICE *continues alone. The lights* **dim** *slowly to darkness. The curtain falls on the scene.*]

27 ANNE'S VOICE: You could not do this and you could not do that. They forced Father out of his business. We had to wear yellow stars. I had to turn in my bike. I couldn't go to a Dutch school any more. I couldn't go to the movies, or ride in an automobile or even on a streetcar, and a million other things. But somehow we children still managed to have fun. Yesterday Father told me we were going into hiding. Where, he wouldn't say. At five o'clock this morning Mother woke me and told me to hurry and get dressed. I was to put on as many clothes as I could. It would look too **suspicious** if we walked along carrying suitcases. It wasn't until we were on our way that I learned where we were going. Our hiding place was to be upstairs in the building where Father used to have his business. Three other people were coming in with us—the Van Daans and their son Peter. Father knew the Van Daans but we had never met them.

28 [During the last lines the curtain rises on the scene. The lights dim on. ANNE'S VOICE fades out.]

Excerpted from *The Diary of Anne Frank: A Play* by Frances Goodrich and Albert Hackett, published by Nelson Thornes Ltd.

Please note that excerpts and passages in the StudySync® library and this workbook are intended as touchstones to generate interest in an author's work. The excerpts and passages do not substitute for the reading of entire texts, and StudySync® strongly recommends that students seek out and purchase the whole literary or informational work in order to experience it as the author intended. Links to online resellers are available in our digital library. In addition, complete works may be ordered through an authorized reseller by filling out and returning to StudySync® the order form enclosed in this workbook.

Reading & Writing Companion   21

First Read

Read *The Diary of Anne Frank: A Play*. After you read, complete the Think Questions below.

☁ THINK QUESTIONS

1. Why do you think Mr. Frank breaks down crying when he picks up the woman's white glove? Use evidence from the text to support your answer.

2. Why is Mr. Frank grateful to Miep? Use evidence from the text to support your answer.

3. How is Anne's diary introduced in the play? What does she describe? Cite evidence to explain your answer.

4. Find the word **trace** in paragraph 3 of *The Diary of Anne Frank: A Play*. Use context clues in the surrounding sentences, as well as the sentence in which the word appears, to determine the word's meaning. Write your definition here and identify clues that helped you figure out its meaning.

5. Use context clues to determine the meaning of **abruptly** as it is used in paragraph 5 of *The Diary of Anne Frank: A Play*. Write your definition here and identify clues that helped you figure out the meaning. Then check the meaning in a dictionary.

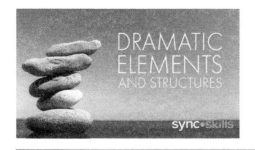

Skill: Dramatic Elements and Structure

Use the Checklist to analyze Dramatic Elements and Structure in *The Diary of Anne Frank: A Play*. Refer to the sample student annotations about Dramatic Elements and Structure in the text.

••• CHECKLIST FOR DRAMATIC ELEMENTS AND STRUCTURE

In order to determine how to compare and contrast the structures of two or more dramatic texts, note the following:

- ✓ the form of the drama, such as comedy or tragedy

- ✓ the characters and setting(s) by act and scene

- ✓ the setting of the play and whether or how it changes in each act and scene

- ✓ the overall structures in the scenes and how they connect to the scenes' meanings

- ✓ the stage directions used

- ✓ the style of language, including verse or other formal language

- ✓ how the acts and scenes advance the plot

- ✓ the dialogue, setting, and plot that contribute to the style of the scene

- ✓ ways the structures of both texts are similar and different

To compare and contrast the structures of two or more texts and analyze how the structure of each text contributes to its meaning and style, use the following questions:

- ✓ How does each author introduce the characters?

- ✓ How do the settings in each drama contribute to the meaning of each text?

- ✓ How does the way the text is structured in each drama contribute to the style? Is the style formalized, as with iambic pentameter? Is the style meant to be realistic?

- ✓ How does the author's use of language in each drama contribute to each text's meaning?

- ✓ How does the choice of structure affect the overall meaning of each drama? How do they compare?

Skill: Dramatic Elements and Structure

Reread lines 23–27 of *The Diary of Anne Frank: A Play* and paragraphs 1–3 of *Anne Frank: The Diary of a Young Girl.* Then, using the Checklist on the previous page, answer the multiple-choice questions below.

⟳ YOUR TURN

1. Based on the stage directions in line 24 of the play, the reader can conclude that—

   ○ A. Anne joins Mr. Frank onstage.
   ○ B. Mr. Frank is reading Anne's words.
   ○ C. Anne's voice is louder than Mr. Frank's.
   ○ D. Mr. Frank is remembering something Anne said.

2. Act I of the play opens with Mr. Frank and his life after the war. Based on the stage directions in line 26, the reader can conclude that—

   ○ A. Mr. Frank will not appear again in Act I.
   ○ B. the first act has concluded.
   ○ C. the rest of Act I will most likely feature Anne telling her own story.
   ○ D. Mr. Frank stops reading the diary.

3. How does the excerpt from *Anne Frank: The Diary of a Young Girl* differ from the drama about the same topic?

   ○ A. Anne's diary goes into detail and provides more information than her dialogue in the play.
   ○ B. Anne's diary is less suspenseful and drives the plot less than her dialogue in the play.
   ○ C. Anne's diary leaves more to the imagination and inference than her dialogue in the play.
   ○ D. Anne's diary reveals other individuals' points of view better than her dialogue in the play.

Skill:
Word Meaning

Use the Checklist to analyze Word Meaning in *The Diary of Anne Frank: A Play.* Refer to the sample student annotations about Word Meaning in the text.

••• CHECKLIST FOR WORD MEANING

In order to find the pronunciation of a word or determine or clarify its precise meaning or its part of speech, do the following:

✓ determine the word's part of speech

✓ consult general and specialized reference materials, both print and digital, to find the pronunciation of a word or determine or clarify its precise meaning or its part of speech

In order to verify the preliminary determination of the meaning of a word or phrase, do the following:

✓ use context clues to make an inference about the word's meaning

✓ consult a dictionary to verify your preliminary determination of the meaning

✓ be sure to read all of the definitions, and then decide which definition makes sense within the context of the text

To determine a word's precise meaning or part of speech, ask the following questions:

✓ What is the word describing?

✓ How is the word being used in the phrase or sentence?

✓ Have I consulted my reference materials?

Skill:
Word Meaning

Reread line 18 of *The Diary of Anne Frank: A Play*. Then, using the Checklist on the previous page, answer the multiple-choice questions below.

↻ YOUR TURN

1. This question has two parts. First, answer Part A. Then, answer Part B.

    Part A: What does the word **rubbish** mean as used in the context of line 18?

    ○ A. furniture
    ○ B. souvenirs
    ○ C. litter
    ○ D. belongings

    Part B: Review the dictionary definitions of the word *rubbish* below.

    rub·bish \'rub ish/
    noun

    1. trash; litter
    2. something worthless
    3. foolish talk; nonsense

    verb

    1. [*British informal*] to criticize as worthless; to attack verbally

    After deciding the context of the word in Part A, which definition best matches *rubbish* as it is used in line 18?

    ○ A. noun definition 1
    ○ B. noun definition 2
    ○ C. noun definition 3
    ○ D. verb definition 1

Close Read

Reread *The Diary of Anne Frank: A Play.* As you reread, complete the Skills Focus questions below. Then use your answers and annotations from the questions to help you complete the Write activity.

◎ SKILLS FOCUS

1. Identify a stage direction that describes Mr. Frank's actions, and explain what those actions reveal about the character.

2. Identify dialogue that gives the audience important background information, and explain how that dialogue helps develop the plot of the excerpt.

3. In *Anne Frank: The Diary of a Young Girl,* Anne Frank describes her family's fear and shock as they prepared to go into hiding. Identify details that reflect strong emotions in the first scene of Act I of *The Diary of Anne Frank: A Play*, and explain how they are similar to and different from the emotions in Anne Frank's diary.

4. Find an unfamiliar word in the text and use context clues to infer its meaning. Then consult a dictionary or other reference material to find its pronunciation and identify its precise meaning.

5. In *Anne Frank: The Diary of a Young Girl*, Anne describes daily life for Jewish people during World War II. Identify and explain details in the opening scene of Act I of *The Diary of Anne Frank: A Play* that show how Anne and her family reacted during this time of crisis.

✏ WRITE

COMPARE AND CONTRAST: In this first scene of Act I of *The Diary of Anne Frank: A Play*, the playwrights include stage directions to show a man, Mr. Frank, preparing to leave. Following that model, choose one brief part of the diary excerpt from *Anne Frank: The Diary of a Young Girl* to dramatize. Following your dramatization, compare the diary excerpt with your drama and also with the play excerpt that you read. How can drama bring out or stress specific ideas? What ideas might be better suited to a diary?

Please note that excerpts and passages in the StudySync® library and this workbook are intended as touchstones to generate interest in an author's work. The excerpts and passages do not substitute for the reading of entire texts, and StudySync® strongly recommends that students seek out and purchase the whole literary or informational work in order to experience it as the author intended. Links to online resellers are available in our digital library. In addition, complete works may be ordered through an authorized reseller by filling out and returning to StudySync® the order form enclosed in this workbook.

Parallel Journeys

INFORMATIONAL TEXT
Eleanor Ayer
1995

Introduction

Parallel Journeys weaves together the stories of two young Germans—Alfons Heck (1928–2005), an enthusiastic participant in the Hitler Youth, and Helen Waterford (b. 1909), a Jewish girl who flees to Holland to avoid persecution by the Nazis, only to be captured and sent to Auschwitz, a concentration camp in German-occupied Poland. Partially narrated in the protagonists' own words, the book serves as a warning against hatred and discrimination and offers an uplifting message about peace and understanding. The excerpt here focuses on recollections of *Kristallnacht*, the Night of Broken Glass.

"It was *Kristallnacht*, the night of broken glass."

from Chapter 4: *Kristallnacht*: The Night of Broken Glass

1   On the afternoon of November 9, 1938, we were on our way home from school when we ran into small troops of SA and SS men[1], the Brownshirts and the Blackshirts. We watched open-mouthed as the men jumped off trucks in the marketplace, fanned out in several directions, and began to smash the windows of every Jewish business in Wittlich[2].

2   Paul Wolff, a local carpenter who belonged to the SS, led the biggest troop, and he pointed out the locations. One of their major targets was Anton Blum's shoe store next to the city hall. Shouting SA men threw hundreds of pairs of shoes into the street. In minutes they were snatched up and carried home by some of the town's nicest families—folks you never dreamed would steal anything.

3   It was *Kristallnacht,* the night of broken glass. For Jews all across Europe, the dark words of warning hurled about by the Nazis suddenly became very real. Just two weeks earlier, thousands of Polish Jews living in Germany had been arrested and shipped back to Poland in boxcars. Among them was the father of seventeen-year-old Herschel Grynszpan, a German Jew who was living in France. Outraged by the Nazis' treatment of his family, Herschel walked into the German Embassy in Paris and shot Ernst vom Rath, the secretary.

4   The murder spawned a night of terror. It was the worst pogrom—the most savage attack against the Jews of Germany—thus far in the twentieth century. Leading the attack was the brutal, boorish SS—the *Schutzstaffel.* On their uniforms, SS members wore **emblems** shaped like double lightening bolts, perfect **symbols** of the terror and suddenness with which they swooped from the night to arrest their frightened victims.

---

1. **SA and SS men** members of paramilitary organizations under Adolf Hitler and the Nazis, and later throughout German-occupied Europe during World War II, which were responsible for enforcing Nazi policies
2. **Wittlich** a town in Southwest Germany

Skill: Informational Text Elements

In these paragraphs, Alfons Heck describes the events of Kristallnacht in a calm, unemotional manner. It is the kind of account you might find in a history book. He reports the facts but does not make any personal judgments about what took place.

5 Heading the *Schutzstaffel* was Heinrich Himmler who worshipped Adolf Hitler. Himmler was a man of great organizational skills, with a passion for perfect record keeping and a heart as black as his *Schutzstaffel* uniform. His power in the *Reich*[3] was tremendous; only Hitler reigned above him.

6 Working under Himmler to carry out the savagery of *Kristallnacht* was Reinhard Heydrich, the number-two man in the SS. His victims dubbed him "The Blond Beast." Even Hitler called him the man with the iron heart. On direct orders from Heydrich, Jewish homes and businesses were destroyed and synagogues burned. "**Demonstrations**," the SS called the violence, and they informed police that they were to do nothing to stop them.

7 "As many Jews, especially rich ones, are to be arrested as can be **accommodated** in the prisons," the orders read. Immediately officials at the concentration camps—the special prisons set up by the Nazis—were **notified** that Jews would be shipped there right away. SS men stormed the streets and searched the attics of Jewish homes, throwing their victims onto trucks to be hauled off to the camps.

8 Four or five of us boys followed Wolff's men when they headed up the *Himmeroder Strasse* toward the Wittlich synagogue. Seconds later the beautiful lead crystal window above the door crashed into the street, and pieces of furniture came flying through doors and windows. A shouting SA man climbed to the roof and waved the rolls of the Torah, the sacred Jewish religious scrolls. "Use it for toilet paper, Jews," he screamed. At that, some people turned shamefacedly away. Most of us stayed, as if riveted to the ground, some grinning evilly.

9 It was horribly brutal, but at the same time very exciting to us kids. "Let's go in and smash some stuff," urged my buddy Helmut. With shining eyes, he bent down, picked up a rock and fired it toward one of the windows. I don't know if I would have done the same thing seconds later, but at that moment my Uncle Franz grabbed both of us by the neck, turned us around and kicked us in the seat of the pants. "Get home, you two *Schweinhunde*," he yelled. "What do you think this is, some sort of circus?"

10 Indeed, it was like a beastly, **bizarre** circus of evil. All across Germany the scene was the same. Terror rained down upon the Jews as Nazis took to the streets with axes, hammers, grenades, and guns. According to reports from high Nazi officials, some 20,000 Jews were arrested, 36 killed, and another 36 seriously injured. Thousands of Jews were hauled to concentration camps during *Kristallnacht*. There many died or were beaten severely by Nazi guards who used this chance to take revenge on a hated people.

• • •

3. **Reich** referring to the German empire

  Reading & Writing Companion

11 Across Europe, Jews panicked as news of the horrors of *Kristallnacht* reached them. In Amsterdam, Helen and Siegfried got their first reports in a phone call from Helen's family.

12 My hometown of Frankfurt, with its 35,000 Jews, had four synagogues. The pogrom started with the burning of the synagogues and all their sacred contents. Jewish stores were destroyed and the windows shattered.

13 Nearly every house was searched for Jewish men. The SA, in plain clothes, came to my parents' apartment to arrest my father and eighteen-year-old brother. A "helpful" neighbor had shown them where in the roomy attic Jews might be hiding. My brother was deported to Buchenwald—a concentration camp near Weimar in eastern Germany— as was Siegfried's brother, Hans.

14 It was not enough for the Jews to suffer destruction of their homes and businesses, beatings and arrests by the SS, and deportation to concentration camps. The Nazis now ordered that the victims must pay for the loss of their own property. The bill for broken glass alone was five million marks. Any insurance money that the Jews might have claimed was taken by the government. And because many of the buildings where Jews had their shops were actually owned by Aryans, the Jews as a group had to pay an additional fine "for their abominable crimes, etc." So declared Hermann Goring, a high-ranking Nazi who was in charge of the German economy. He set their fine at one *billion* marks.

15 For the Jews still left in Germany, the future looked very grim. Many had fled, like Helen and Siegfried, after the first ominous rumblings from Hitler's government. But thousands still remained. These people simply refused to believe that conditions would get any worse. They thought the plight of the Jews would improve, if only they were patient. Helen's father was among them.

16 Although he had lost his business, he was still stubbornly optimistic about the future of the Jews in Germany. Earlier in the summer of 1938 he had been arrested, for no particular reason, and sent to Buchenwald. At that time it was still possible to get people out of a camp if they had a visa to another country. Siegfried and I got permission from the Dutch government for him to come to Holland, but he did not want to leave Germany without his wife and son. Since they had no visas, he stayed with them and waited—until it was almost too late.

Excerpted from *Parallel Journeys* by Eleanor Ayer, published by Aladdin Paperbacks.

Skill: Informational Text Elements

The Waterford family were victims of *Kristallnacht* rather than just observers, but there are connections between the two accounts. Helen, however, makes personal judgments. She mentions a "helpful" neighbor who told the SA where Jews could be found.

First Read

Read *Parallel Journeys*. After you read, complete the Think Questions below.

THINK QUESTIONS

1. What images does the word *Kristallnacht,* or its English translation, "night of broken glass," bring to mind? What words and phrases do the three narrators of the selection—Alfons, Helen, and the author—use that help you form mental pictures of the events happening across Germany on the night of November 9, 1938? Use specific details from the excerpt to support your response.

2. Use details from the text to explain what happened in Germany on *Kristallnacht.*

3. Why did *Kristallnacht* happen? Support your answer, including any inferences you make, with textual evidence.

4. Use context clues in the excerpt to determine the meaning of the word **bizarre** as it appears in paragraph 10. Write your definition of *bizarre* here and explain how you arrived at it.

5. Read the following dictionary entry:

accommodate
ac•com•mo•date \ə'kämə'dāt\ *verb*

1. to do a favor or kindness for someone
2. to provide with housing
3. to have enough room for
4. to adapt to or fit in

Which definition most closely matches the meaning of **accommodate** in paragraph 7? Write the correct definition of *accommodate* here and explain how you figured it out.

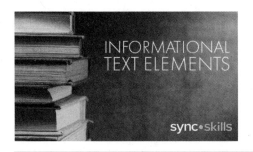

Skill:
Informational Text Elements

Use the Checklist to analyze Informational Text Elements in *Parallel Journeys*. Refer to the sample student annotations about Informational Text Elements in the text.

••• CHECKLIST FOR INFORMATIONAL TEXT ELEMENTS

In order to determine how a text makes connections among and distinctions between individuals, ideas, or events, note the following:

- ✓ key details in the text that describe or explain important ideas, events, or individuals

- ✓ connections, as well as distinctions, between different individuals, ideas, and events, such as:

  - particular characteristics

  - shared experiences

  - similar or different ideas

  - important conversations

- ✓ analogies the author uses to determine the similarities between two pieces of information (e.g., a heart and a pump)

- ✓ comparisons the author makes between individuals, ideas, or events

To analyze how a text makes connections among and distinctions between individuals, ideas, or events, consider the following questions:

- ✓ What kinds of connections and distinctions does the author make in the text?

- ✓ Does the author include any analogies or comparisons? What do they add to the text?

- ✓ What other features, if any, help readers analyze the events, ideas, or individuals in the text?

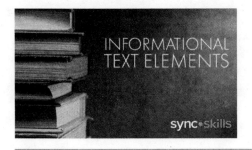

Skill:
Informational Text Elements

Reread paragraphs 9 and 10 of *Parallel Journeys*. Then, using the Checklist on the previous page, answer the multiple-choice questions below.

⟳ YOUR TURN

1. What analogy is made in these two paragraphs, and why?

   ○ A. An analogy is made between the unruly behavior of people on *Kristallnacht* and the noisy and confused behavior that can be found in a circus, because the events taking place are brutal and evil, but also chaotic.

   ○ B. People are running back and forth committing acts of violence, and Alfons compares them to clowns in a circus, running around the Big Top.

   ○ C. Uncle Franz thinks *Kristallnacht* is a circus of evil, and for this reason he does not want Alfons or his friend Helmut to watch it.

   ○ D. Uncle Franz and Alfons think *Kristallnacht* is a circus of evil because some 20,000 Jews were arrested, 36 killed, and another 36 seriously injured.

2. What distinction is made between Alfons's first reaction of the events of *Kristallnacht* in paragraph 9 and his notes about the consequences of the night in paragraph 10?

   ○ A. While Alfons was watching the events of *Kristallnacht,* he did not know that this event was taking place all over Germany.

   ○ B. Alfons thought about throwing a rock, but then his Uncle Franz stopped him and told him to go home.

   ○ C. Although Alfons's friend Helmut threw a rock at a window, there is a distinction between Helmut's act and the axes and hammers used by the Nazis.

   ○ D. Alfons first says *Kristallnacht* was "very exciting to us kids," and then he notes the "terror" and that 20,000 people were imprisoned and others died.

Close Read

Reread *Parallel Journeys*. As you reread, complete the Skills Focus questions below. Then use your answers and annotations from the questions to help you complete the Write activity.

◎ SKILLS FOCUS

1. Explain how the author makes both connections and distinctions between what Alfons and Helen experienced during *Kristallnacht*. Cite textual evidence to support your response.

2. Identify examples that show how the author uses multiple points of view, and explain how these points of view contribute to the text. Cite textual evidence to support your response.

3. Identify connections between the events that occurred in Wittlich on *Kristallnacht* and the events that occurred in Frankfurt, and what this shows about how *Kristallnacht* was planned and organized.

4. Identify details that reveal when the author uses a cause-and-effect text structure. Explain how that text structure develops the key concepts in the text.

5. *Kristallnacht* was a crisis for the Jews and many other people in Germany. Explain how Alfons, Helmut, Uncle Franz, and Helen behaved during this crisis and what this reveals about their characters.

✏ WRITE

NARRATIVE: Write an imagined newspaper account of the events discussed in the excerpt from *Parallel Journeys*. Identify people and places, as well as the relationship between them, as a reporter might. Be careful not to alter the events as you read about them in the selection.

Please note that excerpts and passages in the StudySync® library and this workbook are intended as touchstones to generate interest in an author's work. The excerpts and passages do not substitute for the reading of entire texts, and StudySync® strongly recommends that students seek out and purchase the whole literary or informational work in order to experience it as the author intended. Links to online resellers are available in our digital library. In addition, complete works may be ordered through an authorized reseller by filling out and returning to StudySync® the order form enclosed in this workbook.

Reading & Writing Companion   35

Blood, Toil, Tears and Sweat

INFORMATIONAL TEXT
Winston Churchill
1940

Introduction

In 1939, Great Britain found itself at war with Germany after the Nazi invasion of Poland. Hitler's army was raging across Europe, and British Prime Minister Neville Chamberlain was forced to resign. The First Lord of the Admiralty, Winston Churchill (1874–1965), a soldier and longtime critic of Chamberlain, took over as prime minister. In this first speech as prime minister before Parliament in May of 1940, Churchill resolves to win the war by whatever means necessary. Inspiring the people of the United Kingdom to fight on, he borrows words first uttered in English by Theodore Roosevelt: "I have nothing to offer but blood, toil, tears and sweat."

"I have nothing to offer but blood, toil, tears and sweat."

1 I beg to move,

2 That this House welcomes the formation of a Government representing the united and inflexible resolve of the nation to prosecute the war with Germany to a victorious conclusion.

3 On Friday evening last I received His Majesty's commission to form a new **Administration**. It was the evident wish and will of Parliament[1] and the nation that this should be conceived on the broadest possible basis and that it should include all parties, both those who supported the late Government and also the parties of the Opposition. I have completed the most important part of this task.

 Skill: Informational Text Structure

Churchill acts quickly. He was given the power to make changes in the government less than a week before this speech. He has already made important appointments. He's using time order words to inform people of his actions.

4 A War Cabinet has been formed of five Members, representing, with the Opposition Liberals, the unity of the nation. The three party Leaders have agreed to serve, either in the War Cabinet or in high executive office. The three Fighting Services have been filled. It was necessary that this should be done in one single day, on account of the extreme urgency and **rigour** of events. A number of other positions, key positions, were filled

Sir Winston Churchill gives his first speech as prime minister to the House of Commons "Blood, Toil, Tears and Sweat," 1940.

yesterday, and I am submitting a further list to His Majesty to-night. I hope to complete the appointment of the principal Ministers during to-morrow. The appointment of the other Ministers usually takes a little longer, but I trust that, when Parliament meets again, this part of my task will be completed, and that the administration will be complete in all respects.

---

1. **Parliament** the supreme legislative body of the United Kingdom and the British Overseas Territories

5 I considered it in the public interest to suggest that the House should be summoned to meet today. Mr. Speaker agreed, and took the necessary steps, in accordance with the powers conferred upon him by the Resolution of the House. At the end of the proceedings today, the **Adjournment** of the House will be proposed until Tuesday, 21st May, with, of course, **provision** for earlier meeting, if need be. The business to be considered during that week will be notified to Members at the earliest opportunity. I now invite the House, by the Motion[2] which stands in my name, to record its approval of the steps taken and to declare its confidence in the new Government.

6 To form an Administration of this scale and complexity is a serious undertaking in itself, but it must be remembered that we are in the preliminary stage of one of the greatest battles in history, that we are in action at many other points in Norway and in Holland, that we have to be prepared in the Mediterranean, that the air battle is continuous and that many preparations, such as have been indicated by my hon. Friend below the Gangway, have to be made here at home. In this crisis I hope I may be pardoned if I do not address the House at any length today. I hope that any of my friends and colleagues, or former colleagues, who are affected by the political reconstruction, will make allowance, all allowance, for any lack of ceremony with which it has been necessary to act. I would say to the House, as I said to those who have joined this government: "I have nothing to offer but blood, toil, tears and sweat."

7 We have before us an ordeal of the most grievous kind. We have before us many, many long months of struggle and of suffering. You ask, what is our policy? I can say: It is to wage war, by sea, land and air, with all our might and with all the strength that God can give us; to wage war against a monstrous tyranny, never surpassed in the dark, lamentable catalogue of human crime. That is our policy.

8 You ask, what is our aim? I can answer in one word: It is victory, victory at all costs, victory in spite of all terror, victory, however long and hard the road may be; for without victory, there is no survival. Let that be realised; no survival for the British Empire, no survival for all that the British Empire has stood for, no survival for the urge and impulse of the ages, that mankind will move forward towards its goal. But I take up my task with **buoyancy** and hope. I feel sure that our cause will not be suffered to fail among men. At this time I feel entitled to claim the aid of all, and I say, "come then, let us go forward together with our united strength."

Skill: Informational Text Structure

Churchill repeats the words colleagues and allowance. He's emphasizing these words to persuade people to accept his changes and to unite. His words "blood, toil, tears and sweat" appeal to the senses. They show his own commitment.

---

2. **Motion** a formal proposal for an action in a meeting or court proceeding

First Read

Read "Blood, Toil, Tears and Sweat." After you read, complete the Think Questions below.

☁ THINK QUESTIONS

1. At the beginning of the speech, what does Winston Churchill say he needs the government to accomplish? Why is Churchill making this request? Cite textual evidence to explain your understanding.

2. According to paragraphs 3 and 4 of the excerpted speech, what has Winston Churchill been doing since becoming Prime Minister? Cite textual evidence to explain your understanding.

3. What mood does Churchill convey as he moves through his speech? Use textual evidence to explain how Churchill achieves it.

4. Use context to determine the meaning of the word **provision** as it is used in paragraph 5 of the speech. Write your definition of *provision* here and tell how you found it.

5. The Latin prefix *ad-* means "toward," and the root *jour* comes from French, meaning "day." The Latin suffix *-ment* turns a word into a noun, and it has to do with an action or a process. Based on this knowledge of roots and affixes, write your definition of **adjournment** as it is used in paragraph 5. Be sure to explain how you figured it out.

Please note that excerpts and passages in the StudySync® library and this workbook are intended as touchstones to generate interest in an author's work. The excerpts and passages do not substitute for the reading of entire texts, and StudySync® strongly recommends that students seek out and purchase the whole literary or informational work in order to experience it as the author intended. Links to online resellers are available in our digital library. In addition, complete works may be ordered through an authorized reseller by filling out and returning to StudySync® the order form enclosed in this workbook.

Reading & Writing Companion   **39**

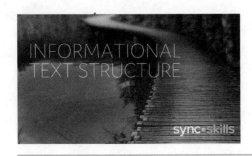

Skill:
Informational Text Structure

Use the Checklist to analyze Informational Text Structure in "Blood, Toil, Tears and Sweat." Refer to the sample student annotations about Informational Text Structure in the text.

••• CHECKLIST FOR INFORMATIONAL TEXT STRUCTURE

In order to determine the structure of a specific paragraph in a text, note the following:

- ✓ details and signal words that reveal the text structure in a paragraph of the text

- ✓ a key concept in the paragraph that is revealed by the text structure the author has chosen to organize the text

- ✓ particular sentences in the paragraph and the role they play in defining and refining a key concept

To analyze in detail the structure of a specific paragraph in a text, including the role of particular sentences in developing and refining a key concept, consider the following questions:

- ✓ What is the structure of the paragraph?

- ✓ Which particular sentences in the paragraph reveal the text structure the author is using?

- ✓ What role do these sentences play in developing and refining a key concept?

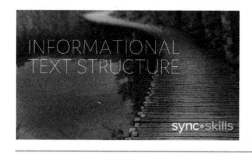

Skill:
Informational Text Structure

Reread paragraphs 7 and 8 from "Blood, Toil, Tears and Sweat." Then, using the Checklist on the previous page, answer the multiple-choice questions below.

⟳ YOUR TURN

1. Based on Churchill's words in paragraph 7, you can conclude that the text structure is meant to—

   - ○ A. narrate in sequential order the events that led to his becoming prime minister.
   - ○ B. persuade others that war must be waged as a solution to the country's problems.
   - ○ C. compare and contrast details that support the policy.
   - ○ D. describe in detail the difficulties to come.

2. Which sentence best represents the key concept of Churchill's speech?

   - ○ A. "We have before us an ordeal of the most grievous kind."
   - ○ B. "We have before us many, many long months of struggle and of suffering. "
   - ○ C. "I feel sure that our cause will not be suffered to fail among men."
   - ○ D. "At this time I feel entitled to claim the aid of all, and I say, 'come then, let us go forward together with our united strength.'"

Please note that excerpts and passages in the StudySync® library and this workbook are intended as touchstones to generate interest in an author's work. The excerpts and passages do not substitute for the reading of entire texts, and StudySync® strongly recommends that students seek out and purchase the whole literary or informational work in order to experience it as the author intended. Links to online resellers are available in our digital library. In addition, complete works may be ordered through an authorized reseller by filling out and returning to StudySync® the order form enclosed in this workbook.

Reading & Writing Companion   41

Close Read

Reread "Blood, Toil, Tears and Sweat." As you reread, complete the Skills Focus questions below. Then use your answers and annotations from the questions to help you complete the Write activity.

◎ SKILLS FOCUS

1. Identify signal words that show how Winston Churchill uses text structure in the first part of "Blood, Toil, Tears and Sweat." Cite evidence to explain why you think Churchill used this text structure.

2. Winston Churchill's language changes in the second half of "Blood, Toil, Tears and Sweat." Identify details in his use of description and repetition. Explain how he develops and refines his key concept and how the text structure supports it.

3. Identify Winston Churchill's claim about World War II in "Blood, Toil, Tears and Sweat." Explain his argument in support of his claim. Cite evidence from his speech.

4. Great Britain was in crisis when Winston Churchill became prime minister. Churchill's response to the crisis in "Blood, Toil, Tears and Sweat" showed what kind of person he was. Explain what you learn about Churchill from this speech and how it affects your view of him as a leader.

✏ WRITE

INFORMATIVE: What information does Winston Churchill present in this speech to Britain? How does the structure of his speech help him develop and refine the key concept of the speech? Cite evidence from the text to explain.

Farewell to Manzanar

INFORMATIONAL TEXT
Jeanne Wakatsuki Houston
and James D. Houston
1973

Introduction

Co-author Jeanne Wakatsuki was seven years old on December 7, 1941, the day Japan bombed the U.S. military base at Pearl Harbor. Not long after, Jeanne and her family, residents of Long Beach, California, were forcibly removed by the Federal Bureau of Investigation (FBI) and incarcerated in internment camps. By the time Japan surrendered in August of 1945, more than 10,000 Japanese Americans had been imprisoned. In her memoir *Farewell to Manzanar*, Wakatsuki remembers her childhood in one of the many internment camps.

"There was no explanation. No one had ever seen anything like this before."

NOTES

from Chapter One: What is Pearl Harbor?

Skill: Textual Evidence

This paragraph tells about Papa's interests. I can see that The Nereid, his boat, "was his pride." The author also describes her father as someone who was a leader because he liked to think everyone "was under his command." He even liked to be called "Skipper"!

1   On that first weekend in December there must have been twenty or twenty-five boats getting ready to leave. I had just turned seven. I remember it was Sunday because I was out of school, which meant I could go down to the wharf and watch. In those days—1941—there was no smog around Long Beach. The water was clean, the sky a sharp Sunday blue, with all the engines of that white sardine fleet puttering up into it, and a lot of yelling, especially around Papa's boat. Papa loved to give orders. He had attended military school in Japan until the age of seventeen, and part of him never got over that. My oldest brothers, Bill and Woody, were his crew. They would have to check the nets again, and check the fuel tanks again, and run back to the grocery store for some more cigarettes, and then somehow everything had been done, and they were easing away from the wharf, joining the line of boats heading out past the lighthouse, into the harbor.

2   Papa's boat was called *The Nereid*—long, white, low-slung, with a foredeck wheel cabin[1]. He had another smaller boat, called *The Waka* (a short version of our name), which he kept in Santa Monica, where we lived. But *The Nereid* was his pride. It was worth about $25,000 before the war, and the way he stood in the cabin steering toward open water you would think the whole fleet was under his command. Papa had a mustache then. He wore knee-high rubber boots, a rust-colored turtleneck Mama had knitted him, and a black skipper's[2] hat. He liked to hear himself called "Skipper."

3   Through one of the big canneries he had made a deal to pay for *The Nereid* with percentages of each catch, and he was anxious to get it paid off. He didn't much like working for someone else if he could help it. A lot of fishermen around San Pedro Harbor had similar contracts with the canneries[3]. In typical Japanese fashion, they all wanted to be independent commercial fishermen,

---

1. **foredeck wheel cabin** a cabin on the forward part of the ship containing the steering mechanism
2. **skipper's** a captain of a ship or boat
3. **canneries** factories where food (often fish) is canned

yet they almost always fished together. They would take off from Terminal Island, help each other find the schools of sardine, share nets and radio equipment--competing and cooperating at the same time.

4   You never knew how long they'd be gone, a couple of days, sometimes a week, sometimes a month, depending on the fish. From the wharf we waved goodbye—my mother, Bill's wife, Woody's wife Chizu, and me. We yelled at them to have a good trip, and after they were out of earshot and the sea had swallowed their engine noise, we kept waving. Then we just stood there with the other women, watching. It was a kind of duty, perhaps a way of adding a little good luck to the voyage, or warding off the bad. It was also marvelously warm, almost summery, the way December days can be sometimes in southern California. When the boats came back, the women who lived on Terminal Island would be rushing to the canneries. But for the moment there wasn't much else to do. We watched until the boats became a row of tiny white gulls on the horizon. Our vigil would end when they slipped over the edge and disappeared. You had to squint against the glare to keep them sighted, and with every blink you expected the last white speck to be gone.

5   But this time they didn't disappear. They kept floating out there, suspended, as if the horizon had finally become what it always seemed to be from shore: the sea's limit beyond which no man could sail. They floated a while, then they began to grow, tiny gulls becoming boats again, a white armada cruising toward us.

6   "They're coming back," my mother said.

7   "Why would they be coming back?" Chizu said.

8   "Something with the engine."

9   "Maybe somebody got hurt."

10   "But they wouldn't *all* come back," Mama said, bewildered.

11   Another woman said, "Maybe there's a storm coming."

12   They all glanced at the sky, scanning the unmarred horizon. Mama shook her head. There was no explanation. No one had ever seen anything like this before. We watched and waited, and when the boats were still about half a mile off the lighthouse, a fellow from the cannery came running down to the wharf shouting that the Japanese had just bombed Pearl Harbor.

13   Chizu said to Mama, "What does he mean? What is Pearl Harbor?"

Skill:
Textual Evidence

I can infer that something is about to change because the boats didn't disappear on the horizon like they usually do. I know this because the narrator writes "but this time they didn't disappear." When the author says that they "began to grow," I can infer that the boats are coming back and something is wrong. Chizu's question supports my analysis that something's wrong. No one expects them to be coming back so soon.

14 Mama yelled at him, "What is Pearl Harbor?"

15 But he was running along the docks, like Paul Revere, bringing the news, and didn't have time to explain.

16 That night Papa burned the flag he had brought with him from Hiroshima thirty-five years earlier. It was such a beautiful piece of material, I couldn't believe he was doing that. He burned a lot of papers too, documents, anything that might suggest he still had some connection with Japan. The precautions didn't do him much good. He was not only an alien; he held a commercial fishing license, and in the early days of the war the FBI was picking up all such men, for fear they were somehow making contact with enemy ships off the coast. Papa himself knew it would only be a matter of time.

17 They got him two weeks later, when we were staying overnight at Woody's place, on Terminal Island. Five hundred Japanese families lived there then, and FBI deputies had been questioning everyone, ransacking houses for anything that could **conceivably** be used for signaling planes or ships or that indicated loyalty to the Emperor. Most of the houses had radios with a short-wave band and a high aerial on the roof so that the wives could make contact with the fishing boats during the long cruises. To the FBI every radio owner was a potential **saboteur**. The confiscators were often deputies sworn in hastily during the **turbulent** days right after Pearl Harbor, and these men seemed to be acting out the general panic, seeing sinister possibilities in the most ordinary household items.

18 If Papa were trying to avoid arrest, he wouldn't have gone near that island. But I think he knew it was **futile** to hide out or resist. The next morning two FBI men in fedora hats and trench coats—like out of a thirties movie—knocked on Woody's door, and when they left, Papa was between them. He didn't struggle. There was no point. He had become a man without a country. The land of his birth was at war with America; yet after thirty-five years here he was still prevented by law from becoming an American citizen. He was suddenly a man with no rights who looked exactly like the enemy.

19 About all he had left at this point was his tremendous dignity. He was tall for a Japanese man, nearly six feet, lean and hard and healthy-skinned from the sea. He was over fifty. Ten children and a lot of hard luck had worn him down, had worn away most of the arrogance he came to this country with. But he still had that dignity, and he would not let those deputies push him out the door. He led them.

20 Mama knew they were taking all alien men first to an interrogation center right there on the island. Some were simply being questioned and released. In the beginning she wasn't too worried; at least she wouldn't let herself be.

Copyright © BookheadEd Learning, LLC

NOTES

But it grew dark and he wasn't back. Another day went by and we still had heard nothing. Then word came that he had been taken into **custody** and shipped out. Where to, or for how long? No one knew. All my brothers' attempts to find out were fruitless.

21 What had they charged him with? We didn't know either, until an article appeared in the Santa Monica paper, saying he had been arrested for delivering oil to Japanese submarines offshore.

22 My mother began to weep. It seems now that she wept for days. She was a small plump woman who laughed and cried easily, but I had never seen her cry like this. I couldn't understand it. I remember clinging to her legs, wondering why everyone was crying. This was the beginning of a terrible, frantic time for all my family.

Excerpted from *Farewell to Manzanar* by Jeanne Wakatsuki Houston and James D. Houston, published by Ember.

Please note that excerpts and passages in the StudySync® library and this workbook are intended as touchstones to generate interest in an author's work. The excerpts and passages do not substitute for the reading of entire texts, and StudySync® strongly recommends that students seek out and purchase the whole literary or informational work in order to experience it as the author intended. Links to online resellers are available in our digital library. In addition, complete works may be ordered through an authorized reseller by filling out and returning to StudySync® the order form enclosed in this workbook.

Reading & Writing Companion   47

First Read

Read *Farewell to Manzanar*. After you read, complete the Think Questions below.

☁ THINK QUESTIONS

1. Based on his attitude toward fishing, what can you infer about Papa's personality? Cite textual evidence to explain your answer.

2. What metaphor do the authors use to describe the fleet of boats heading out into the ocean?

3. Why does Papa burn the Japanese flag? Cite textual evidence to explain.

4. Many words contain the Latin root *turb*, which means "to stir up" or "cause commotion." Use this information to determine the meaning of **turbulent** as it is used in paragraph 17 of the excerpt. In your own words, write a definition of *turbulent* here.

5. Use context to determine the meaning of **futile** as it used in paragraph 18. Write your definition of *futile* here and explain how you figured it out.

Skill:
Textual Evidence

Use the Checklist to analyze Textual Evidence in *Farewell to Manzanar*. Refer to the sample student annotations about Textual Evidence in the text.

••• CHECKLIST FOR TEXTUAL EVIDENCE

In order to support an analysis by citing textual evidence that is explicitly stated in the text, do the following:

- ✓ read the text closely and critically

- ✓ identify what the text says explicitly

- ✓ find the most relevant textual evidence that supports your analysis

- ✓ consider why an author explicitly states specific details and information

- ✓ cite the specific words, phrases, sentences, or paragraphs from the text that support your analysis

- ✓ cite evidence from the text that most strongly supports your analysis

In order to interpret implicit meanings in a text by making inferences, do the following:

- ✓ combine information directly stated in the text with your own knowledge, experiences, and observations

- ✓ cite the specific words, phrases, sentences, or paragraphs from the text that support this inference

In order to cite textual evidence to support an analysis of what the text says explicitly as well as inferences drawn from the text, consider the following questions:

- ✓ Have I read the text closely and critically?

- ✓ What inferences am I making about the text? What textual evidence am I using to support these inferences?

- ✓ Am I quoting the evidence from the text correctly?

- ✓ Does my textual evidence logically relate to my analysis?

- ✓ What textual evidence most strongly supports my analysis?

Copyright © BookheadEd Learning, LLC

Skill:
Textual Evidence

Reread paragraphs 17 and 18 of *Farewell to Manzanar*. Then, using the Checklist on the previous page, answer the multiple-choice questions below.

↻ YOUR TURN

1. What does the text explicitly state in paragraph 17?

   ○ A. The FBI was ransacking Japanese families' homes.
   ○ B. The FBI gave radios to all Japanese families living near the fishing boats.
   ○ C. Papa signaled planes and ships.
   ○ D. Papa went to hide on Terminal Island.

2. This question has two parts. First, answer Part A. Then, answer Part B.

   Part A: What inference can you make about the phrase "He had become a man without a country" in paragraph 18?

   ○ A. Papa wanted to become an American citizen, but he needed to take a test first.
   ○ B. Papa was frustrated that he still wasn't granted citizenship in America after thirty-five years.
   ○ C. Papa wants to return to his birth country of Japan.
   ○ D. Even though Papa lived in America, he was being treated like the enemy because he was Japanese and born in Japan.

   Part B: What line from the text most strongly supports your answer to Part A?

   ○ A. "But I think he knew it was futile to hide out or resist."
   ○ B. "He didn't struggle. There was no point."
   ○ C. "He was suddenly a man with no rights who looked exactly like the enemy."
   ○ D. "If Papa were trying to avoid arrest, he wouldn't have gone near that island."

Close Read

Reread *Farewell to Manzanar.* As you reread, complete the Skills Focus questions below. Then use your answers and annotations from the questions to help you complete the Write activity.

◎ SKILLS FOCUS

1. Cite specific evidence from the text that supports the conclusion that the Wakatsuki family was negatively affected after the bombing of Pearl Harbor.

2. An author's purpose is his or her reasons for writing. Identify an important detail that reveals the authors' purpose in *Farewell to Manzanar,* and explain what that purpose is.

3. Identify an important detail that helps you determine the meaning of the text, and explain how it develops the authors' main idea.

4. Identify a detail that shows Papa's reaction to the events that took place following the bombing of Pearl Harbor. Explain what this reaction says about who Papa is during a crisis.

✏ WRITE

DISCUSSION: Choose one moment in this excerpt from *Farewell to Manzanar* where you can make an inference. What is the inference, and how can it help readers better understand the text? Identify textual evidence that most strongly supports your analysis. Then share and discuss your inference with a small group. In your discussion, be sure to reflect on and adjust your responses as new evidence is presented.

Please note that excerpts and passages in the StudySync® library and this workbook are intended as touchstones to generate interest in an author's work. The excerpts and passages do not substitute for the reading of entire texts, and StudySync® strongly recommends that students seek out and purchase the whole literary or informational work in order to experience it as the author intended. Links to online resellers are available in our digital library. In addition, complete works may be ordered through an authorized reseller by filling out and returning to StudySync® the order form enclosed in this workbook.

Reading & Writing Companion   **51**

Nobel Prize Acceptance Speech

INFORMATIONAL TEXT
Elie Wiesel
1986

Introduction

Elie Wiesel (1928–2016) was a survivor of the Auschwitz and Buchenwald Nazi concentration camps, and went on to write 57 books about the Holocaust and other subjects. Wiesel was awarded the Nobel Peace Prize for his work and accomplishments in 1986. The Nobel Committee heralded Wiesel as one of the world's "most important spiritual leaders" at a time when "terror, repression, and racial discrimination still exist in the world." The following is an excerpt from his Nobel Peace Prize acceptance speech.

"Because if we forget, we are guilty, we are accomplices."

1 And it is with a profound sense of humility that I accept the honor—the highest there is—that you have chosen to **bestow** upon me. I know your choice transcends my person.

2 Do I have the right to represent the multitudes who have perished? Do I have the right to accept this great honor on their behalf? I do not. No one may speak for the dead, no one may interpret their mutilated dreams and visions. And yet, I sense their presence. I always do—and at this moment more than ever. The presence of my parents, that of my little sister. The presence of my teachers, my friends, my companions . . .

3 This honor belongs to all the survivors and their children and, through us to the Jewish people with whose destiny I have always identified.

4 I remember: it happened yesterday, or eternities ago. A young Jewish boy discovered the Kingdom of Night[1]. I remember his **bewilderment**, I remember his **anguish.** It all happened so fast. The ghetto. The deportation. The sealed cattle car.

1986 Nobel Peace Prize winner and writer Elie Wiesel gives a speech after awarding ceremonies on December 11, 1986.

The fiery altar upon which the history of our people and the future of mankind were meant to be sacrificed.

5 I remember he asked his father: "Can this be true? This is the twentieth century, not the Middle Ages. Who would allow such crimes to be committed? How could the world remain silent?"

6 And now the boy is turning to me. "Tell me," he asks, "what have you done with my future, what have you done with your life?"

 Skill: Informational Text Structure

The text becomes sequential. Wiesel describes the horror he experienced as a young boy, and then he moves to the present as he has a conversation with that boy. The adult's answer to the boy's questions conveys a key concept in paragraph 7—we must remember the Holocaust.

---

1. **Kingdom of Night** Elie Wiesel's description of life as a Jewish person under the Nazis during World War II, alluding to the title of his unforgettable memoir, *Night*

 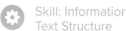

NOTES

7   And I tell him that I have tried. That I have tried to keep memory alive, that I have tried to fight those who would forget. Because if we forget, we are guilty, we are accomplices.

8   And then I explain to him how naïve we were, that the world did know and remained silent. And that is why I swore never to be silent whenever wherever human beings endure suffering and humiliation. We must take sides. Neutrality helps the oppressor, never the victim. Silence encourages the tormentor, never the tormented. Sometimes we must interfere. When human lives are endangered, when human dignity is in jeopardy, national borders and sensitivities become irrelevant. Wherever men or women are **persecuted** because of their race, religion, or political views, that place must—at that moment—become the center of the universe. . .

Skill: Reasons and Evidence

Wiesel supports his claim by referencing people in history who have stood up to injustice and made a difference. These examples are relevant evidence to his claim and help make his argument complete.

9   There is so much to be done, there is so much that can be done. One person—a Raoul Wallenberg[2], an Albert Schweitzer[3], Martin Luther King, Jr.—one person of **integrity**, can make a difference, a difference of life and death.

10 As long as one dissident is in prison, our freedom will not be true. As long as one child is hungry, our life will be filled with anguish and shame. What all these victims need above all is to know that they are not alone; that we are not forgetting them, that when their voices are stifled we shall lend them ours, that while their freedom depends on ours, the quality of our freedom depends on theirs.

11 This is what I say to the young Jewish boy wondering what I have done with his years. It is in his name that I speak to you and that I express to you my deepest gratitude as one who has emerged from the Kingdom of Night. We know that every moment is a moment of grace, every hour an offering; not to share them would mean to betray them.

12 Our lives no longer belong to us alone; they belong to all those who need us desperately.

Copyright © BookheadEd Learning, LLC

2. **Raoul Wallenberg** a Swedish architect, businessman, diplomat, and humanitarian who saved tens of thousands of Jews in Nazi-occupied Hungary during the Holocaust
3. **Albert Schweitzer** a French theologian, writer, philosopher, and physician who won the Nobel Peace Prize in 1952

First Read

Read "Nobel Prize Acceptance Speech." After you read, complete the Think Questions below.

☁ THINK QUESTIONS

1. Who is the young boy who "discovered the Kingdom of Night" in paragraph 4? Use evidence from the text and your knowledge of Wiesel's history to support your answer.

2. What does Wiesel mean when he says in paragraph 7, "Because if we forget, we are guilty, we are accomplices"? Use evidence from the text to support your answer.

3. Write two or three sentences about what Wiesel is calling on his listeners to do. What responsibility does he give to those who listen? Support your answer with textual evidence.

4. Use context clues to determine the meaning of the word **persecuted** as it is used in paragraph 8. Write your best definition of *persecuted* here and explain how you figured it out.

5. Read the following dictionary entry:

integrity

in•teg•ri•ty \in 'te-grə-dē\ *noun*

1. the state of being of sound or solid construction
2. the state of having strong moral principles
3. unity or togetherness

Which definition most closely matches the meaning of **integrity** in paragraph 9? Write the correct definition of *integrity* here and explain how you figured it out.

Please note that excerpts and passages in the StudySync® library and this workbook are intended as touchstones to generate interest in an author's work. The excerpts and passages do not substitute for the reading of entire texts, and StudySync® strongly recommends that students seek out and purchase the whole literary or informational work in order to experience it as the author intended. Links to online resellers are available in our digital library. In addition, complete works may be ordered through an authorized reseller by filling out and returning to StudySync® the order form enclosed in this workbook.

Reading & Writing Companion **55**

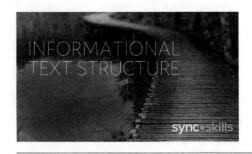

Skill:
Informational Text Structure

Use the Checklist to analyze Informational Text Structure in "Nobel Prize Acceptance Speech." Refer to the sample student annotations about Informational Text Structure in the text.

••• CHECKLIST FOR INFORMATIONAL TEXT STRUCTURE

In order to determine the structure of a specific paragraph in a text, note the following:

✓ details and signal words that reveal the text structure in a paragraph of the text

✓ a key concept in the paragraph that is revealed by the text structure the author has chosen to organize the text

✓ particular sentences in the paragraph and the role they play in defining and refining a key concept

To analyze in detail the structure of a specific paragraph in a text, including the role of particular sentences in developing and refining a key concept, consider the following questions:

✓ What is the structure of the paragraph?

✓ What particular sentences in the paragraph reveal the text structure the author is using?

✓ What role do these sentences play in developing and refining a key concept?

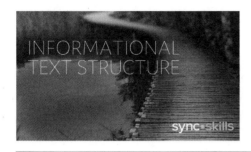

Skill:
Informational Text Structure

Reread paragraphs 8–12 of "Nobel Prize Acceptance Speech." Then, using the Checklist on the previous page, answer the multiple-choice questions below.

⟳ YOUR TURN

1. What text structure does Wiesel use in paragraph 8?

   ○ A. sequential
   ○ B. problem and solution
   ○ C. cause and effect
   ○ D. comparison and contrast

2. Wiesel includes examples in paragraph 9 mainly to make the point that—

   ○ A. Martin Luther King Jr. was a great leader.
   ○ B. thanks to three men, there is little persecution today.
   ○ C. each individual can work to bring about change.
   ○ D. people should work together to make a difference.

3. Which paragraph best shows that Wiesel is thankful for surviving the Holocaust and wants to dedicate the time he was given to help others?

   ○ A. 9
   ○ B. 10
   ○ C. 11
   ○ D. 12

Skill:
Reasons and Evidence

Use the Checklist to analyze Reasons and Evidence in "Nobel Prize Acceptance Speech." Refer to the sample student annotations about Reasons and Evidence in the text.

••• CHECKLIST FOR REASONS AND EVIDENCE

In order to identify the reasons and evidence that support an author's or speaker's claim(s) in an argument, note the following:

✓ the argument the author/speaker is making

✓ the claim or the main idea of the argument

✓ the reasons and evidence that support the claim

✓ whether the evidence the author/speaker presents to support the claim is complete and comprehensive

✓ whether the author/speaker introduces irrelevant evidence, or evidence that is unrelated to the claim and does not support it

To assess whether the reasoning is sound and the evidence is relevant and sufficient, consider the following questions:

✓ What kind of argument is the author/speaker making?

✓ Is the reasoning, or the thinking behind the claims, sound and valid?

✓ Are the reasons and evidence presented to support the claim sufficient, or is more evidence needed? Why or why not?

✓ Does the author/speaker introduce irrelevant evidence that is unrelated to the claim? How do you know?

Skill:
Reasons and Evidence

Reread paragraphs 1–3 of "Nobel Prize Acceptance Speech." Then, using the Checklist on the previous page, answer the multiple-choice questions below.

⟳ YOUR TURN

1. What claim is the speaker making in this passage?

   ○ A. Only those who suffered through the Holocaust can speak for those who did not survive.
   ○ B. The honor belongs to all Jewish people and survivors of the Holocaust, not himself.
   ○ C. The award he is receiving should actually go to those who perished in the Holocaust.
   ○ D. His family, teachers, friends, and companions deserve the award more than he does.

2. Which of the following is a relevant reason that supports the claim from question 1?

   ○ A. "I accept the honor—the highest there is—that you have chosen to **bestow** upon me."
   ○ B. "I have the right to represent the multitudes who have perished."
   ○ C. "I sense their presence. I always do—and at this moment more than ever."
   ○ D. "No one may speak for the dead, no one may interpret their mutilated dreams and visions."

3. Which of the following reasons would **not** be relevant to the author's claim in this passage?

   ○ A. Wiesel says he does not have the right to represent those who perished.
   ○ B. Wiesel cannot accept an honor on behalf of those who died.
   ○ C. Wiesel maintains that no one can speak for the dead.
   ○ D. Wiesel tells his young self that he tried to keep the memory of those who died alive.

NOBEL PRIZE
ACCEPTANCE SPEECH
BY ELIE WIESEL

Close Read

Reread "Nobel Prize Acceptance Speech." As you reread, complete the Skills Focus questions below. Then use your answers and annotations from the questions to help you complete the Write activity.

◎ SKILLS FOCUS

1. Identify details that show how the text structure contributes to the key concept of Elie Wiesel's "Nobel Prize Acceptance Speech." Explain how the details help you understand Wiesel's commitment to work for freedom.

2. Identify reasons and evidence that support Wiesel's claim that "Silence encourages the tormentor, never the tormented." Explain Wiesel's argument.

3. Identify a detail about the crisis that Wiesel faced when he was a boy. Explain how the memory shaped him as a person and motivated the work he did in the years afterward.

✏ WRITE

ARGUMENTATIVE: How does Wiesel connect his personal story to the key concept of this speech? Are his reasons and evidence relevant and effective in developing the speech's message? Support your writing with evidence from the text.

Refugee

FICTION
Alan Gratz
2017

Introduction

While he initially envisioned *Refugee* as three separate narratives, a life-changing trip to Florida convinced author Alan Gratz (b. 1972) to unite the three narratives together into one epic novel. *Refugee's* parallel narratives are set in different times but united by common threads throughout, suggesting that cultures and personalities are not always as dissimilar as they may appear. In this

"Mahmoud Bishara was invisible, and that's exactly how he wanted it. Being invisible was how he survived."

Skill: Language, Style, and Audience

The author uses the word *you*. It feels like the narrator is speaking directly to me, and it pulls me into the story to see Mahmoud. The author also uses words and phrases to describe the dangerous situation that Mahmoud is in daily.

MAHMOUD

ALEPPO, SYRIA—2015

1   Mahmoud Bishara was invisible, and that's exactly how he wanted it. Being invisible was how he survived.

2   He wasn't literally invisible. If you really looked at Mahmoud, got a glimpse under the hoodie he kept pulled down over his face, you would see a twelve-year-old boy with a long, strong nose, thick black eyebrows, and short-cropped black hair. He was stocky, his shoulders wide and muscular despite the food shortages. But Mahmoud did everything he could to hide his size and his face, to stay under the radar. Random death from a fighter jet's missile or a soldier's rocket launcher might come at any moment, when you least expected it. To walk around getting noticed by the Syrian army or the rebels fighting them was just inviting trouble.

3   Mahmoud sat in the middle row of desks in his classroom, where the teacher wouldn't call on him. The desks were wide enough for three students at each, and Mahmoud sat between two other boys named Ahmed and Nedhal.

4   Ahmed and Nedhal weren't his friends. Mahmoud didn't have any friends.

5   It was easier to stay invisible that way.

6   One of the teachers walked up and down the hall ringing a handbell, and Mahmoud collected his backpack and went to find his little brother, Waleed.

7   Waleed was ten years old and two grades below Mahmoud in school. He too wore his black hair cropped short, but he looked more like their mother, with narrower shoulders, thinner eyebrows, a flatter nose, and bigger ears. His teeth looked too big for his head, and when he smiled he looked like a cartoon squirrel. Not that Waleed smiled much anymore. Mahmoud couldn't remember the last time he'd seen his brother laugh, or cry, or show any emotion whatsoever.

8   The war had made Mahmoud nervous. Twitchy. **Paranoid**. It had made his little brother a robot.

9   Even though their apartment wasn't far away, Mahmoud led Waleed on a different route home every day. Sometimes it was the back alleys; there could be fighters in the streets, who were always targets for the opposition. Bombed-out buildings were good too. Mahmoud and Waleed could disappear among the heaps of twisted metal and broken cement, and there were no walls to fall on them if an artillery shell went whizzing overhead. If a plane dropped a barrel bomb, though, you needed walls. Barrel bombs were filled with nails and scrap metal, and if you didn't have a wall to duck behind you'd be shredded to pieces.

10   It hadn't always been this way. Just four years ago, their home city of Aleppo had been the biggest, brightest, most modern city in Syria. A crown jewel of the Middle East. Mahmoud remembered neon malls, glittering skyscrapers, soccer stadiums, movie theaters, museums. Aleppo had history too—a long history. The Old City, at the heart of Aleppo, was built in the 12th century, and people had lived in the area as early as 8,000 years ago. Aleppo had been an amazing city to grow up in.

11   Until 2011, when the Arab Spring came to Syria.

12   They didn't call it that then. Nobody knew a wave of **revolutions** would sweep through the Middle East, toppling governments and overthrowing dictators and starting civil wars. All they knew from images on TV and posts on Facebook and Twitter was that people in Tunisia and Libya and Yemen were rioting in the streets, and as each country stood up and said "Enough!" so did the next one, and the next one, until at last the Arab Spring came to Syria.

13   But Syrians knew protesting in the streets was dangerous. Syria was ruled by Bashar al-Assad, who had twice been "elected" president when no one was allowed to run against him. Assad made people who didn't like him disappear. Forever. Everyone was afraid of what he would do if the Arab Spring swept through Syria. There was an old Arabic proverb that said, "Close the door that brings the wind and relax," and that's exactly what they did; while the rest of the Middle East was rioting, Syrians stayed inside and locked their doors and waited to see what would happen.

14   But they hadn't closed the door tight enough. A man in Damascus, the capital of Syria, was imprisoned for speaking out against Assad. Some kids in Daraa, a city in southern Syria, were arrested and abused by the police for writing anti-Assad slogans on walls. And then the whole country seemed to go crazy all at once. Tens of thousands of people poured into the streets, demanding the release of political prisoners and more freedom for everyone. Within a

NOTES

Please note that excerpts and passages in the StudySync® library and this workbook are intended as touchstones to generate interest in an author's work. The excerpts and passages do not substitute for the reading of entire texts, and StudySync® strongly recommends that students seek out and purchase the whole literary or informational work in order to experience it as the author intended. Links to online resellers are available in our digital library. In addition, complete works may be ordered through an authorized reseller by filling out and returning to StudySync® the order form enclosed in this workbook.

Reading & Writing Companion   63

month, Assad had turned his tanks and soldiers and bombers on the protestors—on his own *people*—and ever since then, all Mahmoud and Waleed and anyone else in Syria had known was war.

15   Mahmoud and Waleed turned down a different **rubble**-strewn alley than the day before and stopped dead. Just ahead of them, two boys had another boy up against what was left of a wall, about to take the bag of bread he carried.

16   Mahmoud pulled Waleed behind a burned-out car, his heart racing. **Incidents** like this were common in Aleppo lately. It was getting harder and harder to get food in the city. But for Mahmoud, the scene brought back memories of another time, just after the war had begun.

17   Mahmoud had been going to meet his best friend, Khalid. Down a side street just like this one, Mahmoud found Khalid getting beaten up by two older boys. Khalid was a Shia Muslim[1] in a country of mostly Sunni Muslims[2]. Khalid was clever. Smart. Always quick to raise his hand in class, and always with the right answer. He and Mahmoud had known each other for years, and even though Mahmoud was Sunni and Khalid was Shia, that had never mattered to them. They liked to spend their afternoons and weekends reading comic books and watching superhero movies and playing video games.

18   But right then, Khalid had been curled into a ball on the ground, his hands around his head while the older boys kicked him.

19   "Not so smart now, are you, pig?" one of them had said.

20   "Shia should know their place! This is Syria, not Iran!"

21   Mahmoud had **bristled**. The differences between Sunnis and Shiites was an excuse. These boys had just wanted to beat someone up.

22   With a battle cry that would have made Wolverine proud, Mahmoud had launched himself at Khalid's attackers.

23   And he had been beaten up as badly as Khalid.

24   From that day forward, Mahmoud and Khalid were marked. The two older boys became Mahmoud's and Khalid's own personal bullies, delivering repeated beatdowns between classes and after school.

---

1. **Shia** a minority branch of Islam which holds that the Islamic prophet Muhammad designated Ali ibn Abi Talib as his successor—in contrast with the Sunni belief that Muhammad did not appoint a successor
2. **Sunni** the largest denomination of Islam, Sunni Muslims elected Muhammad's father-in-law, Abu Bakr, as the first caliph, believing that the prophet did not appoint a direct successor

25 That's when Mahmoud and Khalid had learned how valuable it was to be invisible. Mahmoud stayed in the classroom all day, never going to the bathroom or the playground. Khalid never answered another question in class, not even when the teacher called on him directly. If the bullies didn't notice you, they didn't hit you. That's when Mahmoud had realized that together, he and Khalid were bigger targets; alone, it was easier to be invisible. It was nothing they ever said to each other, just something they each came to understand, and within a year they had drifted apart, not even speaking to each other as they passed in the hall.

Excerpted from *Refugee* by Alan Gratz, published by Scholastic Press.

Please note that excerpts and passages in the StudySync® library and this workbook are intended as touchstones to generate interest in an author's work. The excerpts and passages do not substitute for the reading of entire texts, and StudySync® strongly recommends that students seek out and purchase the whole literary or informational work in order to experience it as the author intended. Links to online resellers are available in our digital library. In addition, complete works may be ordered through an authorized reseller by filling out and returning to StudySync® the order form enclosed in this workbook.

Reading & Writing Companion   **65**

First Read

Read *Refugee*. After you read, complete the Think Questions below.

 THINK QUESTIONS

1. Why did Mahmoud think that his best defense was to become "invisible"? Were there any other choices he could have made? Cite specific evidence from the text in your response.

2. How does the Arab Spring impact Syria? Were there any noticeable differences in Mahmoud's life before and after it occurred? Be sure to note any positive and negative effects, based on your understanding of the reading.

3. Was there another way for Khalid and Mahmoud to preserve their friendship? Was their only option to stop talking to one another, and did they make the best decision? Why or why not? Use specific evidence from the text in your response.

4. What is the meaning of the word **bristled** as it is used in the text? Write your best definition here, along with a brief explanation of how you arrived at its meaning.

Skill:
Language, Style, and Audience

Use the Checklist to analyze Language, Style, and Audience in *Refugee*. Refer to the sample student annotations about Language, Style, and Audience in the text.

••• CHECKLIST FOR LANGUAGE, STYLE, AND AUDIENCE

In order to determine an author's style, do the following:

- ✓ identify and define any unfamiliar words or phrases

- ✓ use context, including the meaning of surrounding words and phrases

- ✓ note possible reactions to the author's word choice

- ✓ examine your reaction to the author's word choice

- ✓ identify any analogies, or comparisons in which one part of the comparison helps explain the other

To analyze the impact of specific word choices on meaning and tone, ask the following questions:

- ✓ How did your understanding of the language change during your analysis?

- ✓ How do the writer's word choices impact or create meaning in the text?

- ✓ How does the writer's choice of words impact or create a specific tone in the text?

- ✓ How could various audiences interpret this language? What different possible emotional responses can you list?

- ✓ What analogies do you see? Where might an analogy have clarified meaning or created a specific tone?

Please note that excerpts and passages in the StudySync® library and this workbook are intended as touchstones to generate interest in an author's work. The excerpts and passages do not substitute for the reading of entire texts, and StudySync® strongly recommends that students seek out and purchase the whole literary or informational work in order to experience it as the author intended. Links to online resellers are available in our digital library. In addition, complete works may be ordered through an authorized reseller by filling out and returning to StudySync® the order form enclosed in this workbook.

Reading & Writing
Companion

67

Skill:
Language, Style, and Audience

Reread paragraphs 12 and 13 of *Refugee*. Then, using the Checklist on the previous page, answer the multiple-choice questions below.

↻ YOUR TURN

1. What tone does the author set in the second to fourth sentences of paragraph 12?

   ○ A. pleading
   ○ B. romantic
   ○ C. casual
   ○ D. scornful

2. What impact on meaning does *crazy* have in paragraph 14?

   ○ A. It describes how angry people had become.
   ○ B. It reveals that mental illness and anxiety were increasing.
   ○ C. It stresses the total loss of control in the country.
   ○ D. It explains the fear that people were experiencing.

3. Which phrase from the excerpt would most likely cause a reaction of horror in the audience?

   ○ A. "knew protesting in the streets was dangerous"
   ○ B. "afraid of what he would do if the Arab Spring swept through Syria"
   ○ C. "Tens of thousands of people poured into the streets"
   ○ D. "turned his tanks and soldiers and bombers on the protestors—on his own *people*"

Close Read

Reread *Refugee*. As you reread, complete the Skills Focus questions below. Then use your answers and annotations from the questions to help you complete the Write activity.

◎ SKILLS FOCUS

1. Identify an incident in the story that reveals an aspect of Mahmoud's character or that provoked a decision he made.

2. Analyze word choice in the story by identifying a word or phrase that you feel has a strong impact on the meaning or tone, and explain why you think it has this effect.

3. Note and explain details that show how Mahmoud responds to the crisis in his country and in his personal life. How has he changed during a time of crisis?

✎ WRITE

LITERARY ANALYSIS: Which words chosen by the author to describe images, ideas, and events in *Refugee* do you think strongly convey what it is like to be **challenged** by living in the midst of a civil war? Cite textual evidence, including specific word choices that affected you strongly, and explain why they had this effect.

Please note that excerpts and passages in the StudySync® library and this workbook are intended as touchstones to generate interest in an author's work. The excerpts and passages do not substitute for the reading of entire texts, and StudySync® strongly recommends that students seek out and purchase the whole literary or informational work in order to experience it as the author intended. Links to online resellers are available in our digital library. In addition, complete works may be ordered through an authorized reseller by filling out and returning to StudySync® the order form enclosed in this workbook.

Reading & Writing Companion   **69**

America

POETRY
Claude McKay
1921

Introduction

Born in Sunny Ville, Jamaica, Claude McKay (1889–1948) was an important figure in the 1920s literary movement known as the Harlem Renaissance. Although a selection of McKay's prose and poetry depicts the basic joys of peasant life in rural Jamaica, McKay is best known for his fiction and poetry that directly addresses the racism and urban tribulations that black people faced in America during the early twentieth century. A line in one of his most well-known poems, "If We Must Die," perhaps best underscores McKay's style and poetic aims: "Pressed to the wall, dying, but fighting back!"

"I will confess / I love this cultured hell that tests my youth!"

1 Although she feeds me bread of bitterness,
2 And sinks into my throat her tiger's tooth,
3 Stealing my breath of life, I will confess
4 I love this **cultured** hell that tests my youth!
5 Her **vigor** flows like tides into my blood,
6 Giving me strength erect against her hate.
7 Her bigness sweeps my being like a flood.
8 Yet as a rebel fronts a king in state,
9 I stand within her walls with not a shred
10 Of terror, **malice**, not a word of **jeer**.
11 Darkly I gaze into the days ahead,
12 And see her might and granite wonders there,
13 Beneath the touch of Time's **unerring** hand,
14 Like priceless treasures sinking in the sand.

Jamaican writer and poet Claude McKay (1889–1948) in a photograph from the book *Back to Montparnasse* by Sisley Huddleston, published in 1931

✏ WRITE

DISCUSSION: Why do you think McKay refers to America as *she* in his poem? Do you think there is symbolism behind this choice? Discuss these questions with a group of your peers. To prepare for your discussion, set specific goals for sharing everyone's opinion, defining individual roles (speaker, recorder, timer) as needed. Use evidence of his relationship with America from the poem as support for your ideas. After your discussion, you will write a reflection in the space below.

Please note that excerpts and passages in the StudySync® library and this workbook are intended as touchstones to generate interest in an author's work. The excerpts and passages do not substitute for the reading of entire texts, and StudySync® strongly recommends that students seek out and purchase the whole literary or informational work in order to experience it as the author intended. Links to online resellers are available in our digital library. In addition, complete works may be ordered through an authorized reseller by filling out and returning to StudySync® the order form enclosed in this workbook.

Reading & Writing Companion   **71**

Gandhi the Man:
How One Man Changed Himself to Change the World

INFORMATIONAL TEXT
Eknath Easwaran
2011

Introduction

Using methods of nonviolent civil disobedience, including protests and marches, Mahatma Gandhi (1869–1948) led the independence movement that eventually overthrew British rule in India. Later, Gandhi and his followers challenged excessive land taxes, discrimination, and the mistreatment of women, ultimately inspiring people around the world to organize for civil rights. In his heralded biography, *Gandhi the Man: How One Man Changed Himself to Change the World*, Eknath Easwaran tells the story of the remarkable leader. This excerpt focuses on Gandhi's famous Salt March to the sea.

"Gandhi was right: the body might be frail but the spirit was boundless."

Copyright © BookheadEd Learning, LLC

from the Introduction: Gandhi: Then & Now

Growing Up in Gandhi's India

1   I like to say I grew up not in British India but in Gandhi's India, because he dominated my world like a colossus[1]. I was a small boy when he returned after twenty years in South Africa and was hailed as Mahatma, "great soul," in 1915. I was too young (and my little village too isolated) to have much awareness of the tragedies that impelled him into national leadership in those early years. Only when I went to college, at the age of sixteen, did I discover his weekly "viewspaper," *Young India*. Gandhi was pouring his heart out in those pages, and despite the country's widespread **illiteracy**, I daresay his words reached into every one of India's villages as the paper was passed from hand to hand and read out to audiences everywhere along the way.

2   My college years were turbulent ones in Indian affairs. I must have been a junior on the night of December 31, 1929, when at the stroke of midnight the Indian Congress declared independence and **unfurled** the flag of a free India. Its motto, pure Gandhi, came from the most ancient scriptures: *Satyam eva jayate,* "Truth ever conquers." Jawaharlal Nehru said later that on that night "we made a tryst with destiny." Those were thrilling times for a village boy away at college, but they were only the beginning. Like the Americans with their Declaration of Independence, we had also made a tryst with war. But this was to be a war without weapons. In March 1930, Gandhi wrote the British Viceroy that he intended to launch nonviolent resistance by marching to the sea to break a **statute** that made the sale and manufacture of salt a government **monopoly**, adding that he would accept the consequences cheerfully and that he was inviting the rest of India to do the same. That letter, the journalist Louise Fischer observed with pleasure, "was surely the strangest ever received by the head of a government." But the Salt March[2] provided brilliant theater. Gandhi and his small band of volunteers took fourteen days to reach the sea,

---

1. **colossus**   a gigantic statue
2. **Salt March**   an act of civil disobedience which took place from March to April 1930 in India, led by Mahatma Gandhi, to protest British rule in India

stopping at every village along the way and making headlines around the world. By the time he reached the ocean the procession was several thousand strong. When he picked up a handful of sea salt from the beach and raised it as a signal to the rest of India, millions of people around the world must have watched him on the newsreels. But in India nobody needed the media. The country simply exploded in utterly nonviolent disobedience of British law.

3   What no one dared to expect was that in the face of police charges, beatings, arrests, and worse, the nonviolence held. Everyone knew Gandhi would drop the campaign if there was any violence on our part, no matter what the provocation. We "kept the pledge" day after day, filling the jails literally to overflowing. Many veterans of those days recall their terms in prison as the high point of their lives; Gandhi had made "suffering for Truth" a badge of honor.

4   I can't describe the effect this had on me, on all of India. Obviously it was high drama, but most significant for me was the human **alchemy** being wrought. These were ordinary people, family, friends, school chums, acquaintances, men and women we saw daily at the marketplace or at temple, at work or school; all ages, high caste and low, educated and ignorant, cultured and crude, rich beyond calculation and unbelievably poor. How had they suddenly become heroes and heroines, cheerfully stepping forward to be beaten with steel-tipped batons, hauled off to jail, stripped of their livelihoods, sometimes even shot? Called to be more than human, we looked around and saw that we were capable of it. Gandhi was right: the body might be frail but the spirit was boundless. We were much, much stronger than we had thought, capable of great things, not because we were great but because there was divinity in us all—even those who swung the clubs and wielded the guns. For me, the burning question became: What was the secret of this alchemy?

Excerpted from Gandhi the Man: How One Man Changed Himself to Change the World by Eknath Easwaran, published by Nilgiri Press.

WRITE

PERSONAL RESPONSE: In the biography *Gandhi the Man: How One Man Changed Himself to Change the World,* we learn of Gandhi's nonviolent Salt March, in which he inspired thousands of Indian citizens to peacefully protest British law, despite being on the receiving end of violent beatings, arrests, and shootings. As a result, ordinary people became heroes while following the nonviolent and unconventional methods of Gandhi. Think about your own life. When have you used unconventional methods to solve a problem? What was your motivation? What effect did your choices have on the outcome? Support your response with evidence from the text as well as personal experience. As you make connections between Gandhi's motivations and your own, include anything that may have altered your understanding of Gandhi's unconventional methods.

Please note that excerpts and passages in the StudySync® library and this workbook are intended as touchstones to generate interest in an author's work. The excerpts and passages do not substitute for the reading of entire texts, and StudySync® strongly recommends that students seek out and purchase the whole literary or informational work in order to experience it as the author intended. Links to online resellers are available in our digital library. In addition, complete works may be ordered through an authorized reseller by filling out and returning to StudySync® the order form enclosed in this workbook.

Reading & Writing Companion   75

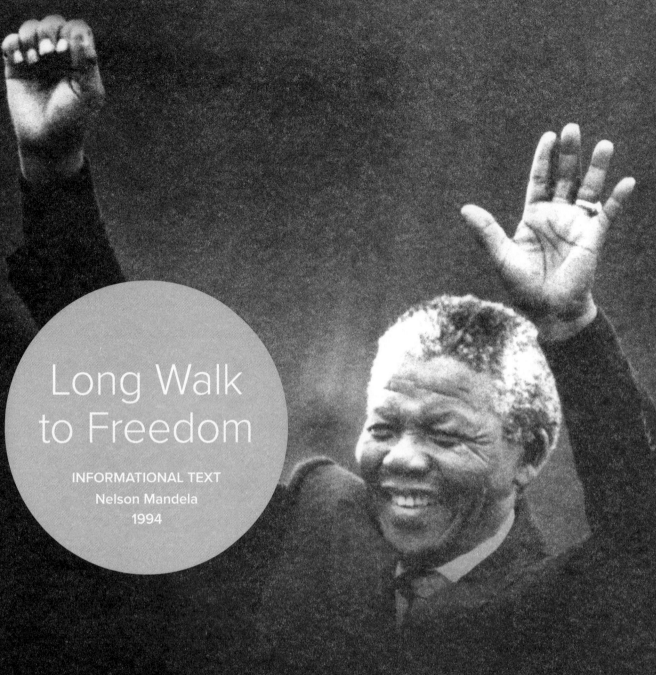

Long Walk to Freedom

INFORMATIONAL TEXT
Nelson Mandela
1994

Introduction

studysync ⓣ

From prisoner to president of South Africa, Nelson Mandela was one of the most important political figures of the 20th century. In 1944, Mandela became a leader in the African National Congress, a political party that opposed South Africa's policy of racial segregation. In 1962, Mandela was jailed for his political activities, and after a widely publicized trial, was sentenced to life in prison. Over the years, Mandela became the world's best-known political prisoner, gaining international support for his fight against apartheid. He was released from captivity in 1990 and went on to become South Africa's first black president. The excerpt here is from Mandela's autobiography titled *Long Walk to Freedom.*

"The brave man is not he who does not feel afraid, but he who conquers that fear."

from Part Eleven: Freedom

NOTES

1 · On the day of the **inauguration**, I was overwhelmed with a sense of history. In the first decade of the twentieth century, a few years after the bitter Anglo-Boer War[1] and before my own birth, the white-skinned peoples of South Africa patched up their differences and erected a system of racial domination against dark-skinned peoples of their own land. The structure they created formed the basis of one of the harshest, most inhumane societies the world has ever known. Now, in the last decade of the twentieth century, and my own eighth decade as a man, that system had been overturned forever and replaced by one that recognized the rights and freedoms of all peoples regardless of the color of their skin.

2 · That day had come about through the unimaginable sacrifices of thousands of my people, people whose suffering and courage can never be counted or repaid. I felt that day, as I have on so many other days, that I was simply the sum of all those African patriots who had gone before me. That long and noble line ended and now began again with me. I was pained that I was not able to thank them and that they were not able to see what their sacrifices had wrought.

3 · The policy of **apartheid** created a deep and lasting wound in my country and my people. All of us will spend many years, if not generations, recovering from that profound hurt. But the decades of oppression and brutality had another, unintended effect, and that was that it produced the Oliver Tambos, the Walter Sisulus, the Chief Luthulis, the Yusuf Dadoos, the Bram Fischers, the Robert Sobukwes of our time—men of such extraordinary courage, wisdom, and generosity that their like may never be known again. Perhaps it requires such depth of oppression to create such heights of character. My country is rich in the minerals and gems that lie beneath its soil, but I have always known that its greatest wealth is its people, finer and truer than the purest diamonds.

Skill: Informational
Text Elements

Mandala compares the
citizens of South
Africa to diamonds in
this analogy because
they are the greatest
wealth to the country,
especially during times
of oppression.

---

1. **Anglo-Boer War** a war fought between the British Empire and two Boer states, the South African Republic and the Orange Free State, over the Empire's influence in South Africa

Skill: Author's Purpose and Point of View

Mandela uses strong words to describe incredibly brave people. He says that even those people felt fear, but what helped them stay strong was determination. I think Mandela's purpose is to inspire that kind of courage in others.

4   It is from these comrades in the struggle that I learned the meaning of courage. Time and again, I have seen men and women risk and give their lives for an idea. I have seen men stand up to attacks and torture without breaking, showing a strength and resiliency that defies the imagination. I learned that courage was not the absence of fear, but the triumph over it. I felt fear myself more times than I can remember, but I hid it behind a mask of boldness. The brave man is not he who does not feel afraid, but he who conquers that fear.

5   I never lost hope that this great **transformation** would occur. Not only because of the great heroes I have already cited, but because of the courage of the ordinary men and women of my country. I always knew that deep down in every human heart, there is mercy and generosity. No one is born hating another person because of the color of his skin, or his background, or his religion. People must learn to hate, and if they can learn to hate, they can be taught to love, for love comes more naturally to the human heart than its opposite. Even in the grimmest times in prison, when my comrades and I were pushed to our limits, I would see a glimmer of humanity in one of the guards, perhaps just for a second, but it was enough to reassure me and keep me going. Man's goodness is a flame that can be hidden but never extinguished.

6   We took up the struggle with our eyes wide open, under no illusion that the path would be an easy one. As a young man, when I joined the African National Congress, I saw the price my comrades paid for their beliefs, and it was high. For myself, I have never regretted my commitment to the struggle, and I was always prepared to face the hardships that affected me personally. But my family paid a terrible price, perhaps too dear a price for my commitment.

7   In life, every man has twin **obligations**—obligations to his family, to his parents, to his wife and children; and he has an obligation to his people, his community, his country. In a civil and humane society, each man is able to fulfill those obligations according to his own inclinations and abilities. But in a country like South Africa, it was almost impossible for a man of my birth and color to fulfill both of those obligations. In South Africa, a man of color who attempted to live as a human being was punished and isolated. In South Africa, a man who tried to fulfill his duty to his people was inevitably ripped from his family and home and was forced to live a life apart, a twilight existence of secrecy and rebellion. I did not in the beginning choose to place my people above my family, but in attempting to serve my people, I found that I was prevented from serving my obligations as a son, a brother, a father, and a husband.

8   In that way, my commitment to my people, to the millions of South Africans I would never know or meet, was at the expense of the people I knew best and loved most. It was as simple and yet as incomprehensible as the moment

a small child asks her father, "Why can you not be with us?" And the father must utter the terrible words: "There are other children like you, a great many of them. . ." and then one's voice trails off.

9   I was not born with a hunger to be free. I was born free—free in every way that I could know. Free to run in the fields near my mother's hut, free to swim in the clear stream that ran through my village, free to roast mealies under the stars and ride the broad backs of slow-moving bulls. As long as I obeyed my father and abided by the customs of my tribe, I was not troubled by the laws of man or God.

10   It was only when I began to learn that my boyhood freedom was an illusion, when I discovered as a young man that my freedom had already been taken from me, that I began to hunger for it. At first, as a student, I wanted freedom only for myself, the transitory freedoms of being able to stay out at night, read what I pleased, and go where I chose. Later, as a young man in Johannesburg, I yearned for the basic and honorable freedoms of achieving my potential, of earning my keep, of marrying and having a family—the freedom not to be obstructed in a lawful life.

11   But then I slowly saw that not only was I not free, but my brothers and sisters were not free. I saw that it was not just my freedom that was curtailed, but the freedom of everyone who looked like I did. That is when I joined the African National Congress, and that is when the hunger for my own freedom became the greater hunger for the freedom of my people to live their lives with dignity and self-respect that animated my life, that transformed a frightened young man into a bold one, that drove a law-abiding attorney to become a criminal, that turned a family-loving husband into a man without a home, that forced a life-loving man to live like a monk. I am not more virtuous or self-sacrificing than the next man, but I found that I could not even enjoy the poor and limited freedoms I was allowed when I knew my people were not free. Freedom is indivisible; the chains on any one of my people were the chains on all of them, the chains on all of my people were the chains on me.

12   It was during those long and lonely years that my hunger for the freedom of my own people became a hunger for the freedom of all people, white and black. I knew as well as I knew anything that the oppressor must be liberated just as surely as the oppressed. A man who takes away another man's freedom is a prisoner of hatred, he is locked behind the bars of prejudice and narrow-mindedness. I am not truly free if I am taking away someone else's freedom, just as surely as I am not free when my freedom is taken from me. The oppressed and the oppressor alike are robbed of their humanity.

13   When I walked out of prison, that was my mission, to liberate the oppressed and the oppressor both. Some say that has now been achieved. But I know

that is not the case. The truth is that we are not yet free; we have merely achieved the freedom to be free, the right not to be oppressed. We have not taken the final step of our journey, but the first step on a longer and even more difficult road. For to be free is not merely to cast off one's chains, but to live in a way that respects and **enhances** the freedom of others. The true test of our devotion to freedom is just beginning.

14　I walked that long road to freedom. I have tried not to falter; I have made missteps along the way. But I have discovered the secret that after climbing a great hill, one only finds that there are many more hills to climb. I have taken a moment here to rest, to steal a view of the glorious vista that surrounds me, to look back on the distance I have come. But I can rest only for a moment, for with freedom comes responsibility, and I dare not linger, for my long walk is not yet ended.

From *Long Walk to Freedom* by Nelson Mandela. Copyright (c) 1994, 1995 by Nelson Rolihlahla Mandela. Reprinted by permission of Little, Brown and Company.

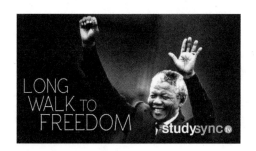

First Read

Read *Long Walk to Freedom*. After you read, complete the Think Questions below.

☁ THINK QUESTIONS

1. Use details from the first paragraph to explain the social and political changes that have taken place in South Africa since the 1990s.

2. Write two or three sentences explaining Mandela's point of view about courage and his own reaction to fear. Support your answer with evidence from paragraph 4.

3. What does Mandela mean by a person's "twin obligations"? Use details stated directly in paragraph 7, as well as ideas you have inferred from clues in the text.

4. Recall that the Latin prefix *trans-* means "across" or "to change completely," and the suffix *-ation* means "act or process." Then use the context clues provided in paragraph 5 to determine the meaning of **transformation.** Write your definition of *transformation* here and tell how you figured out its meaning.

5. Use context clues and word relationships to determine the meaning of the word **enhance** as it is used in paragraph 13 of *Long Walk to Freedom*. Write your definition of *enhance* and tell how you determined its meaning.

Skill: Author's Purpose and Point of View

Use the Checklist to analyze Author's Purpose and Point of View in *Long Walk to Freedom*. Refer to the sample student annotations about Author's Purpose and Point of View in the text.

••• CHECKLIST FOR AUTHOR'S PURPOSE AND POINT OF VIEW

In order to identify author's purpose and point of view, note the following:

- ✓ facts, statistics, and graphic aids, as these indicate that the author is writing to inform

- ✓ the author's use of emotional or figurative language, which may indicate that the author is trying to persuade readers or stress an opinion

- ✓ descriptions that present a complicated process in plain language, which may indicate that the author is writing to explain

- ✓ the language the author uses, such as figurative and emotional language, can be a clue to the author's point of view on a subject or topic

- ✓ whether the author acknowledges and responds to conflicting evidence or points of view that contradict his or her own

To determine the author's purpose and point of view in a text, consider the following questions:

- ✓ How does the author convey, or communicate, information in the text?

- ✓ Does the author use figurative or emotional language? What does this indicate?

- ✓ Are charts, graphs, maps, and other graphic aids included in the text? For what purpose?

- ✓ Does the author acknowledge contradictory or conflicting evidence or other points of view? How does the author respond to or address them?

Skill: Author's Purpose and Point of View

Reread paragraphs 9–12 of *Long Walk to Freedom*. Then, using the Checklist on the previous page, answer the multiple-choice questions below.

↻ YOUR TURN

1. Based on Mandela's discussion of freedom in paragraphs 9–12, the reader can conclude that—

   ○ A. Mandela longed for freedom even as a young boy
   ○ B. Mandela's beliefs about freedom changed over the years.
   ○ C. Mandela's beliefs about freedom came from his family.
   ○ D. Mandela's need for personal freedom became more important when he was an adult.

2. The ideas that Mandela expresses in paragraph 12 reveal he believed—

   ○ A. all people must have freedom.
   ○ B. only criminals should be in prison.
   ○ C. only apartheid limited freedom.
   ○ D. freedom is only an illusion.

Please note that excerpts and passages in the StudySync® library and this workbook are intended as touchstones to generate interest in an author's work. The excerpts and passages do not substitute for the reading of entire texts, and StudySync® strongly recommends that students seek out and purchase the whole literary or informational work in order to experience it as the author intended. Links to online resellers are available in our digital library. In addition, complete works may be ordered through an authorized reseller by filling out and returning to StudySync® the order form enclosed in this workbook.

Reading & Writing Companion 83

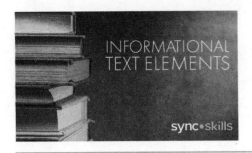

Skill:
Informational Text Elements

Use the Checklist to analyze Informational Text Elements in *Long Walk to Freedom*. Refer to the sample student annotations about Informational Text Elements in the text.

••• CHECKLIST FOR INFORMATIONAL TEXT ELEMENTS

In order to determine how a text makes connections among and distinctions between individuals, ideas, or events, note the following:

✓ key details in the text that describe or explain important ideas, events, or individuals

✓ categories of connections, as well as distinctions, among individuals, ideas, or events such as:

• particular characteristics

• shared experiences

• similar or different ideas

• important conversations

✓ analogies the author uses to determine the similarities between two pieces of information (e.g., a heart and a pump)

✓ comparisons the author makes between individuals, ideas, or events

To analyze how a text makes connections among and distinctions between individuals, ideas, or events, consider the following questions:

✓ What kinds of connections and distinctions does the author make in the text?

✓ Does the author include any analogies or comparisons? What do they add to the text?

✓ What other features, if any, help readers analyze the events, ideas, or individuals in the text?

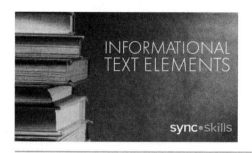

Skill:
Informational Text Elements

Reread paragraph 7 of *Long Walk to Freedom*. Then, using the Checklist on the previous page, answer the multiple-choice questions below.

⟳ YOUR TURN

1. This question has two parts. First, answer Part A. Then, answer Part B.

   Part A: What comparison is Mandela making in this passage

   ○ A. men's ability to meet twin obligations in a civil and humane society versus in South Africa

   ○ B. the obligations men have to family versus the obligations they have to their people

   ○ C. Mandela's experience in fulfilling his obligations versus what other men experienced

   ○ D. men's obligations under apartheid in South Africa versus their obligations after apartheid ended

   Part B: Which of the following quotes from the passage BEST supports your response to Part A?

   ○ A. "In life, every man has twin **obligations**—obligations to his family, to his parents, to his wife and children; and he has an obligation to his people, his community, his country."

   ○ B. "But in a country like South Africa, it was almost impossible for a man of my birth and color to fulfill both of those obligations."

   ○ C. "In South Africa, a man of color who attempted to live as a human being was punished and isolated."

   ○ D. "I did not in the beginning choose to place my people above my family"

Close Read

Reread *Long Walk to Freedom*. As you reread, complete the Skills Focus questions below. Then use your answers and annotations from the questions to help you complete the Write activity.

◎ SKILLS FOCUS

1. Identify a detail in the text that shows Mandela's purpose in writing the autobiography and a detail that shows his point of view. Explain the connection between his purpose and point of view.

2. Identify details in Mandela's argument supporting his claim that "with freedom comes responsibility." Explain why this idea applies not only to South Africans but to people all over the world.

3. Identify and explain how lines in the autobiography show how Mandela connects apartheid, suffering, and oppression to the highest forms of character.

4. Identify examples in *Long Walk to Freedom* that show how anger and fear played a role in Nelson Mandela's life and defined him in a crisis.

✏ WRITE

ARGUMENTATIVE: In the autobiography *Long Walk to Freedom,* what is Nelson Mandela's purpose? How does Mandela communicate his point of view about strength despite living in times of crisis? Cite evidence from the selection to explain.

Extended Oral Project and Grammar

EXTENDED ORAL PROJECT

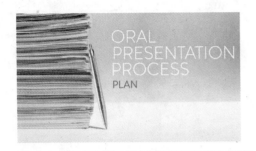

Oral Presentation Process: Plan

PLAN	DRAFT	REVISE	EDIT AND PRESENT

The texts from the *Trying Times* unit show individuals and characters caught in the middle of hardships and tragedies. In reading about their lives, we get to see the issues that matter most to them. Some, like Nelson Mandela, report their feelings directly: "The truth is that we are not yet free; we have merely achieved the freedom to be free, the right not to be oppressed." Others, like Anne Frank, the author of the *Diary of Anne Frank*, share their points of view by describing their experiences. In turn, these texts help us to reflect on our own views of relevant topics.

WRITING PROMPT

How do you advocate a position?

Think about issues that are important to you, and consider what the people and characters you have read about in this unit can teach you about those issues. Taking inspiration from three of those individuals, prepare and deliver a speech in which you advocate a position on a topic you care about. Include claims, reasons, and relevant evidence from your personal experience and the selections to support your position. In your presentation, be sure to employ the following in order to communicate your ideas effectively:

- a clear position on an issue
- a style that appeals to a specific audience
- an emphasis on salient points
- clarity and cohesion
- integration of multimedia and visual displays
- speaking techniques such as adequate volume and clear pronunciation
- body language such as appropriate eye contact

Copyright © BookheadEd Learning, LLC

Introduction to an Oral Presentation

Argumentative oral presentations use engaging writing, body language, and multimedia and visual displays to convince an audience about an issue. Good oral presentations convey important information in an engaging, clear, and coherent way. That requires speakers to craft strong arguments for their audiences, use effective speaking techniques, and strengthen their arguments by using multimedia along with visual displays. The characteristics of argumentative oral presentations include:

- a clear position on an issue
- a style that appeals to a specific audience
- an emphasis on salient points
- clarity and cohesion
- integration of multimedia and visual displays
- speaking techniques such as adequate volume and clear pronunciation
- body language such as appropriate eye contact

As you continue with this Extended Oral Project, you'll receive more instruction and practice in crafting each of these characteristics to create your own oral presentation.

Please note that excerpts and passages in the StudySync® library and this workbook are intended as touchstones to generate interest in an author's work. The excerpts and passages do not substitute for the reading of entire texts, and StudySync® strongly recommends that students seek out and purchase the whole literary or informational work in order to experience it as the author intended. Links to online resellers are available in our digital library. In addition, complete works may be ordered through an authorized reseller by filling out and returning to StudySync® the order form enclosed in this workbook.

Reading & Writing Companion   89

Before you get started on your own argumentative oral presentation, read the oral presentation that one student, Kristen, wrote in response to the writing prompt. As you read the Model, highlight and annotate any features of argumentative oral presentations.

Copyright © BookheadEd Learning, LLC

NOTES

☰ STUDENT MODEL

Truth Be Told

By Kristen F.

Introduction:

Have you ever felt that you had to hide your true feelings to avoid hurting others? I felt like this on the way to a horseback riding competition last year. During the whole drive, my mother talked excitedly about the upcoming show, and I nodded along while smiling. But the truth was that I had started dreading the competitions.

Introduction (Continued):

Since I was 8 years old, I had spent almost every weekend show jumping, a type of horseback riding that involves jumping over obstacles. I enjoyed learning about horses and meeting other riders, but I did not like the competitions. In contrast, my mother looked forward to the competitions, and I could see how proud she felt each time a judge handed me a ribbon. I wished that I had felt as happy as she did during those moments, but I never did. I wanted to be honest with her, but I also did not know how the truth would affect our relationship.

Claim:

What should you do when the truth seems too painful to tell? I knew I had to be honest with my mother, and some selections that we read helped me understand why. Winston Churchill, Elie Wiesel, and Anne Frank are examples of people who had the courage to share difficult truths in much more trying situations. Their words have shown me why I need to share facts that are important for others to know. That information can help them understand a conflict and find ways to respond to it.

What should you do when the truth seems too painful to tell?

- **Examples: Winston Churchill, Elie Wiesel, and Anne Frank**
- **Claim: The truth can help people understand a conflict and find ways to respond to it.**

Evidence and Analysis #1:

Changing many people's attitudes toward a war is a challenge, but Winston Churchill was able to do that in his speech "Blood, Toil, Tears and Sweat."

Please note that excerpts and passages in the StudySync® library and this workbook are intended as touchstones to generate interest in an author's work. The excerpts and passages do not substitute for the reading of entire texts, and StudySync® strongly recommends that students seek out and purchase the whole literary or informational work in order to experience it as the author intended. Links to online resellers are available in our digital library. In addition, complete works may be ordered through an authorized reseller by filling out and returning to StudySync® the order form enclosed in this workbook.

Reading & Writing Companion   91

This is a photo of Churchill in 1940, several months after he made that speech. In May of 1940, Churchill was elected as prime minister of the United Kingdom. The United Kingdom was at war, and Churchill needed to address a devastating defeat. Even though it could not have been easy, Churchill was honest about the situation.

Evidence and Analysis #1 (Continued):

In a historic speech, Churchill announced that this war would involve "many long months of struggle and suffering." However, Churchill then said that this war was for an important cause. The country was fighting to remain free. Promising not to abandon the audience, Churchill also said, "I have nothing to offer but blood, toil, tears and sweat." These words show Churchill's dedication to the cause. This speech demonstrates how to face a crisis with honesty.

"Blood, Toil, Tears and Sweat"

- "many long months of struggle and suffering"
- "I have nothing to offer but blood, toil, tears and sweat."

Evidence and Analysis #2:

The Nazis were one of the governments that the United Kingdom fought, and they were persecuting Jewish people in Europe. From 1941 to 1945, they carried out the Holocaust. The Holocaust was the organized killing of more than six million Jewish people in concentration camps and millions of other people as well.

The Holocaust (1941 to 1945): The Holocaust was the organized killing of more than six-million Jewish people in concentration camps and millions of other people as well.

Evidence and Analysis #2 (Continued):

Elie Wiesel was one of the survivors and my second example of someone who told difficult truths. In 1986, Wiesel received the Nobel Peace Prize. He used the speech to challenge his audience to speak out against evil. Wiesel stated actions that everyone should take. For example, he explained why everyone needs to remember the Holocaust: "That I have tried to keep memory alive, that I have tried to fight those who would forget. Because if we forget, we are guilty, we are accomplices." He also emphasized that human beings around the world are still being persecuted, and we have a responsibility to speak up for them.

Elie Wiesel, Winner of the 1986 Nobel Peace Prize

- "That I have tried to keep memory alive, that I have tried to fight those who would forget. Because if we forget, we are guilty, we are accomplices." —Elie Wiesel

Evidence and Analysis #2 (Continued):

The following video from NBC News is from 1999 and shows Wiesel speaking at the White House. The brave words of Elie Wiesel showed me that although some information can be painful, it is important to know.

Evidence and Analysis #3:

With Wiesel's speech in mind, we can turn to *The Diary of Anne Frank.* This is a photo of Anne Frank writing in 1940. It was taken before she went into hiding and before the Nazis sent her family to a concentration camp. Her father, Otto Frank, was the only person in her family who survived the Holocaust. He edited and published her diaries as a way to make her writing live on after her death.

NOTES

Evidence and Analysis #3 (Continued):

In Anne's diary, she describes hopes, interests, and conflicts. For example, she tries to make her space in the annex seem happier by decorating it with postcards and pictures of movie stars. At the same time, Frank constantly faces the possibility of being found by the Nazis. That information was hard for me to read, but she was sharing facts and details that we need to know. Her words remind me that millions of people had their lives cut short by hatred and war. To make sure that does not happen again, I must advocate for people in need and share truths that are not easy to hear.

Anne's Diary

- Describes her hopes, interests, and conflicts
- Describes living her life despite the possibility of being found by the Nazis
- How I can respond to Anne's diary

Review:

Churchill, Wiesel, and Frank all chose to tell the truth in moments of extreme crisis, and their actions show us how to act in our everyday lives.

Winston Churchill
Elie Wiesel
Anne Frank

Great models for us!

NOTES

Conclusion:

In my own situation, I told my mother my feelings about horseback riding. Though she missed the excitement of shows, she understood that competing is not for everyone. She even helped me find a new hobby: I now volunteer at a ranch that teaches horseback riding to children with disabilities.

What should you do when the truth seems too painful to tell?

- My mother understood.
- I made a leap...

Conclusion (Continued):

Therefore, telling the truth, even when it is hard to do so, is important. Even though some facts can be difficult to learn, they help others deepen or change their understanding of a conflict.

Telling difficult truths is important.

- Facts can help others deepen their understanding of a topic.
- Facts can help people change their opinions or make a difference.

Thank you for listening!

Works Cited

NBC News. "President Bill Clinton and Holocaust survivor Elie Wiesel speak about apathy, involvement, and international-relations as the Twenty-First Century approaches." *NBC News Archives Xpress*, NBCUniversal Media, LLC, 12 April 1999, https://www.nbcnewsarchivesxpress.com/contentdetails/211449.

✏ **WRITE**

Writers often take notes about their arguments before they sit down to write. Think about what you've learned so far about organizing argumentative writing to help you begin prewriting.

- What topic or issue is important to you? What is your position on the issue?

- Based on your personal experience or background knowledge, are there reasons why you support that position?

- Which texts from the year will help you argue your position?

- What relationship do these texts have to your topic or issue?

- What anecdotes from your personal life or background knowledge are relevant to the topic of your presentation?

- What multimedia or visual displays could you use during your presentation? How will they affect your audience?

- What speaking techniques will help you communicate your ideas?

- What body language will help you communicate your ideas?

Response Instructions

Use the questions in the bulleted list to write a one-paragraph summary. Your summary should describe what you will discuss in your oral presentation like the one on the previous pages.

Don't worry about including all of the details now; focus only on the most essential and important elements. You will refer back to this short summary as you continue through the steps of the writing process.

Please note that excerpts and passages in the StudySync® library and this workbook are intended as touchstones to generate interest in an author's work. The excerpts and passages do not substitute for the reading of entire texts, and StudySync® strongly recommends that students seek out and purchase the whole literary or informational work in order to experience it as the author intended. Links to online resellers are available in our digital library. In addition, complete works may be ordered through an authorized reseller by filling out and returning to StudySync® the order form enclosed in this workbook.

Reading & Writing Companion   **97**

Skill: Evaluating Sources

First, reread the sources you gathered and identify the following:

- what kind of source it is, including video, audio, or text, and where the source comes from
- where information seems inaccurate, biased, or outdated
- where information seems irrelevant or incomplete

In order to use advanced searches to gather relevant, credible, and accurate print and digital sources, use the following questions as a guide:

- Is the material published by a well-established source or expert author?
- Is the material up-to-date or based on the most current information?
- Is the material factual, and can it be verified by another source?
- Are there specific terms or phrases in my research question that I can use to adjust my search?
- Can I use "and," "or," or "not" to expand or limit my search?
- Can I use quotation marks to search for exact phrases?

↻ YOUR TURN

Read the sentences below that describe factors about sources. Then, complete the chart by placing them into two categories: those that show a source is credible and reliable and those that do not.

	Factors
A	The article states only the author's personal opinions and omits, or leaves out, other positions.
B	The article includes clear arguments and counterarguments.
C	The text relies on biased information to persuade readers.
D	The text is objective and includes many viewpoints.
E	The website is a personal blog.
F	The author is a reporter for a nationally recognized newspaper.

Credible and Reliable	Not Credible or Reliable

Please note that excerpts and passages in the StudySync® library and this workbook are intended as touchstones to generate interest in an author's work. The excerpts and passages do not substitute for the reading of entire texts, and StudySync® strongly recommends that students seek out and purchase the whole literary or informational work in order to experience it as the author intended. Links to online resellers are available in our digital library. In addition, complete works may be ordered through an authorized reseller by filling out and returning to StudySync® the order form enclosed in this workbook.

Reading & Writing
Companion

99

YOUR TURN

Complete the chart below by filling in the title and author of a source and answering questions about it.

Questions	Answers
Source Title and Author:	
Reliability: Has the source material been published in a well-established book or periodical or on a well-established website?	
Reliability: Is the source material up-to-date or based on the most current information?	
Credibility: Is the source material written by a recognized expert on the topic?	
Credibility: Is the source material published by a well-respected author or organization?	
Bias: Is the source material connected to people or organizations that are objective and unbiased?	
Accuracy: Does the source cite information that is factual and able to be verified?	
Should I use this source in my paper?	

Skill: Organizing an Oral Presentation

In order to present claims and findings using appropriate eye contact, adequate volume, and clear pronunciation, do the following:

- Decide whether your presentation will be delivered to entertain, critique, inform, or persuade.
- Identify your audience in order to create your content.
- Choose a style for your oral presentation, either formal or informal.
- Present claims and the information you have found to support them, emphasizing salient, or relevant and significant, points in a focused, coherent manner.
- Integrate multimedia and visual displays to clarify information, strengthen claims and evidence, and add interest.
- Use appropriate eye contact, adequate volume, and clear pronunciation.

To present claims and findings using appropriate eye contact, adequate volume, and clear pronunciation, consider the following questions:

- Have I decided on the purpose of my presentation and identified my audience?
- Have I chosen a style for my oral presentation, either formal or informal?
- Did I make sure that the descriptions, facts, and details I present are pertinent and support what I have to say?
- Have I emphasized relevant, salient points in a clear, coherent manner?
- Did I integrate multimedia and visual displays to clarify information, strengthen claims and evidence, and add interest?
- Did I practice using appropriate eye contact, adequate volume, and clear pronunciation?

YOUR TURN

Complete the chart by writing a short description of each aspect of your argumentative oral presentation.

Oral Presentation Aspects	Description
Purpose	
Audience	
Style	
Thesis Statement	
Reasons and Relevant Evidence	
Multimedia Components	
Oral Presentation Skills	

✏ **WRITE**

Use the questions in the checklist to outline your oral presentation. Be sure to present your thesis and support for that thesis in a logical order. Your outline should emphasize important points and show how they are connected to one another.

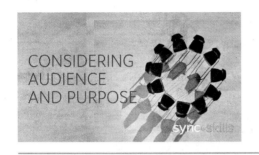

Skill: Considering Audience and Purpose

••• CHECKLIST FOR CONSIDERING AUDIENCE AND PURPOSE

In order to present claims and findings using appropriate eye contact, adequate volume, and clear pronunciation, note the following:

- When writing your presentation, emphasize salient, or relevant and significant, points.
- Present your claims and findings in a clear, coherent manner.
- Produce evidence that is relevant to your claims or findings.
- Use sound, valid reasoning and well-chosen details that support your claim or findings.
- Use adequate eye contact.
- Speak at an adequate volume so you can be heard by everyone.
- Use correct pronunciation.
- Remember to adapt your speech according to your task, and if it is appropriate, use formal English and not language you would use in ordinary conversation.

To better understand how to present claims and findings and use appropriate eye contact, adequate volume, and clear pronunciation, consider the following questions:

- What is the purpose of my presentation?
- What might audience members already know about this topic?
- What might audience members need to know about this topic?
- How can I present my argument in a way that my audience will understand?
- How can I present my argument in a way that will engage my audience?
- What register will be appropriate for my audience?
- What tone will be appropriate for my audience?
- What vocabulary will be appropriate for my audience?
- Will my audience still be able to hear my unique voice in this presentation?

YOUR TURN

Read the quotations from students' presentations below. Then, complete the chart by sorting the quotations into those that use formal language and those that use informal language.

	Quotations
A	Students should be required to wash their hands before lunch in order to avoid flu outbreaks.
B	I think we've all said something we'd later regret, right?
C	Another way that characters influence the plot is through dialogue.
D	I learned to be positive, to help others, and to believe in my abilities.
E	The narrator is totally boring. I don't know why anyone would ever like him.
F	The character looks around, really confused. He's thinking, *This is bad*.

Formal	Informal

YOUR TURN

Complete the chart by considering how you will adjust your presentation based on different audiences. The first example has been completed.

Audience	Adjustments
Students from Grade 5	I will use an informal register. Since audience members may not be familiar with the topic, I will explain background information, and I will define any academic vocabulary that I use.
The United Nations	
Community Leaders	
Experts in a Related Field	
Community Leaders and Students from Grade 5	

Please note that excerpts and passages in the StudySync® library and this workbook are intended as touchstones to generate interest in an author's work. The excerpts and passages do not substitute for the reading of entire texts, and StudySync® strongly recommends that students seek out and purchase the whole literary or informational work in order to experience it as the author intended. Links to online resellers are available in our digital library. In addition, complete works may be ordered through an authorized reseller by filling out and returning to StudySync® the order form enclosed in this workbook.

Reading & Writing Companion   105

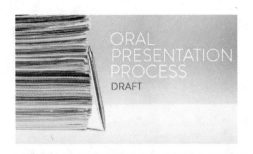

Oral Presentation Process: Draft

PLAN	DRAFT	REVISE	EDIT AND PRESENT

You have already made progress toward writing your argumentative oral presentation. Now it is time to draft your argumentative oral presentation.

✏ WRITE

Use your plan and other responses in your Binder to draft your presentation. You may also have new ideas as you begin drafting. Feel free to explore those new ideas as you have them. You can also ask yourself four questions:

- Have I developed a clear position and considered the best way to share it with my audience?

- Have I developed a clear and cohesive argument?

- Have I integrated multimedia and visual displays into my presentation to clarify information, strengthen claims and evidence, and add interest?

- Have I identified the speaking techniques and body language that I need to work on to communicate my ideas?

Before you submit your draft, read it over carefully. You want to be sure that you've responded to all aspects of the prompt.

Copyright © BookheadEd Learning, LLC

Here is Kristen's oral presentation draft. As you read, identify details that help Kristen grab her audience's attention.

NOTES

☰ STUDENT MODEL: FIRST DRAFT

Telling Difficult Truths

Have you ever felt that you had to hide your true feelings to avoid hurting others? Did you feel sick or wanting to hide? I felt like this on the way to a horseback riding competition last year. During the whole drive, my mom talked excitedly about the upcoming show. She suggested that I tried new techniques, and I nodded along while smiling. But the truth was that I would start disliking competitions.

Since I was 8-years-old, I had spent almost every weekend show jumping, a type of horseback riding that involves jumping over obstacles. I got to learn about horses and meeting other riders, but the pressure to win ribbons made it stressful too. While I was interested in caring for my horse, my mom loved to strategize about how I could beat my fellow riders there. Focused on a win distracted me from my friends and love of riding. My mom had already spent lots of money renting stables, transporting my horse, and to buy my riding gear. It was a big investment, and I could see how proud my mom felt each time a judge handed me a ribbon. I wished that I feel as happy as she did during those moments. I also didn't know how my quitting show jumping will effect our relationship.

What should you do when the truth were to seem to painful to tell? In some of the selections we have read, people have decided to tell the truth in far more trying situations. What do those selections say about sharing difficult truths?

Changing many people's attitudes toward a war is a challenge, but Winston Churchill was able to do that in his speech "Blood, Toil, Tears and Sweat." He had just been elected as Prime Minister of the United Kingdom in 1940, but this was not a moment to celebrate because the United Kingdom was at war. Churchill needed to address a devastated defeat even though that couldn't have been easy, Churchill were honest about the situation. ~~In a historic speech, Churchill said that the war was about to become more difficult.~~

Please note that excerpts and passages in the StudySync® library and this workbook are intended as touchstones to generate interest in an author's work. The excerpts and passages do not substitute for the reading of entire texts, and StudySync® strongly recommends that students seek out and purchase the whole literary or informational work in order to experience it as the author intended. Links to online resellers are available in our digital library. In addition, complete works may be ordered through an authorized reseller by filling out and returning to StudySync® the order form enclosed in this workbook.

Reading & Writing Companion 107

Skill:
Reasons and
Relevant Evidence

Kristen identifies ideas in her presentation that are not developed with evidence and reasons. She focuses on a single claim and adds textual evidence that helps explain her idea.

Skill:
Sources and
Citations

Kristen adds the source of the video to her paragraph. She will include a full citation in her works cited list at the end of her presentation.

~~However, Churchill then emphasized that this war was for an important cause. The country was fighting against fascism. When a government is led by a dictator who strictly controls the nation. Promising not to abandon the audience, the quote, "I have nothing to offer but blood, toil, tears and sweat" was important. Churchill's dedication to the cause is shown by these words. This speech shows how to face a crisis with honesty.~~

In a historic speech, Churchill announced that this war would involve "many long months of struggle and suffering." However, Churchill then said that this war was for an important cause. The country was fighting to remain free. Promising not to abandon the audience, Churchill also said, "I have nothing to offer but blood, toil, tears and sweat." These words show Churchill's dedication to the cause. This speech demonstrates how to face a crisis with honesty.

The Nazis were one of the fascist parties that the United Kingdom would fight, and they were persecuting Jewish people in Europe. From 1941 to 1945 they carried out the Holocaust, the mass killing of over six-million people in concentration camps. Elie Wiesel was one of the survivors, as well as my second example of someone who told difficult truths. In 1986, the distinguished Nobel Peace Prize was received by Wiesel. He used the speech to challenge his audience to speak out against evil. Addressing many powerful people, he clearly stated actions that everyone should take. It does not matter where the crisis is happening or who is being harmed. For example, he explained why everyone needs to remember the Holocaust: "That I have tried to keep memory alive, that I have tried to fight those who would forget. Because if we forget, we are guilty, we are accomplices." He also emphasized that human beings around the world are still being persecuted. Speaking up for them is our responsibility.

~~The following video is from 1999 and shows Wiesel speaking at the White House.~~

The following video from NBC News is from 1999 and shows Wiesel speaking at the White House. The brave words of Elie Wiesel showed me that although some information can be painful, it is important to know.

With Wiesel's speech in mind, we can turn to *The Diary of Anne Frank*.

This is a photo of Anne Frank writing in 1940. It was taken before she went into hiding and before the Nazis sent her family to a concentration camp.

Her father, Otto Frank was the only person in her family who survived the Holocaust. Editing and publishing her diaries as a way to make her writing live on after her death. In Anne's diary, she describes hopes, interests, and conflicts that sound so familure she

Skill:
Communicating Ideas

Kristen decides to add a photo to her presentation. As she speaks, she will use a hand gesture to direct her audience's attention to the photo.

tries to make her space in the Annex seam happier by decorate it with postcards and pictures of movie stars. (I couldn't believe this because my own locker at school is covered with pictures and postcards.) At the same time, Frank constantly faces the possibility of being found by the Nazis. That information was hard for me to read, but she was sharing facts and details that we need to know. Her words remind me that millions of people had their lives cut short by hatred and war. To make sure that does not happen again, I must avocate for people in need and share truths that were not easy to hear.

Churchill, Wiesel, and Frank all chose to tell the truth in moments of extreme crisis. Even though some facts can be difficult to learn, it helps others deepen or change their understanding of a conflict. I told my mom my feelings about horseback riding. Though she missed the excitement of shows, she would understand that competing isn't for everyone. She even helped me find a new hobby volunteering at a ranch that teaches horseback riding to children with disabilities. Both fun and fulfilling, I now have a way to to make a difference. I am happy that I was able to tell my mother how I felt about horseback riding competitions. Churchill Wiesel and Frank are all excellent examples of people who have told the truth when it were not easy. Plus, they remind me that I have a responsibility helping people in my community or anywhere else.

Skill:
Communicating Ideas

••• CHECKLIST FOR COMMUNICATING IDEAS

In order to present claims and findings using appropriate eye contact and body language, adequate volume, and clear pronunciation, note the following:

- When writing your presentation, emphasize salient, or relevant and significant, points.
- Present your claims and findings in a clear, coherent manner.
- Remember to use adequate eye contact and gestures.
- Speak at an adequate volume so you can be heard by everyone.
- Use correct pronunciation.

To better understand how to present claims and findings and use appropriate eye contact and body language, adequate volume, and clear pronunciation, consider the following questions:

- Have I used appropriate eye contact when giving my presentation?
- Did I use an appropriate speaking rate, volume, and enunciation to clearly communicate with my listeners?
- Did I use natural gestures to add meaning and interest as I speak?

YOUR TURN

Below are several examples of students communicating their ideas. Fill in the correct strategy to match each example.

	Strategies
A	Keep your posture
B	Use gestures
C	Make eye contact
D	Speak clearly

Example	Strategy
A student waves his hands in the air when retelling a funny story.	
A student straightens her back when she realizes she is slouching.	
A student changes which audience member she looks at in the middle of her presentation.	
A student speaks loudly because the audience is large.	

WRITE

Take turns reading your presentation aloud to a partner. When you finish, write a reflection about your experience of communicating ideas. How clearly did you speak while giving your presentation? How did you use your speaking rate, volume, and gestures to emphasize your ideas? How can you better communicate your ideas in the future?

When you are presenting:

- Employ steady eye contact to help keep your listeners' attention.

- Use an appropriate speaking rate, volume, and enunciation to clearly communicate with your listeners.

- Use natural gestures to add meaning and interest as you speak.

- Keep in mind conventions of language, and avoid informal or slang speech.

Please note that excerpts and passages in the StudySync® library and this workbook are intended as touchstones to generate interest in an author's work. The excerpts and passages do not substitute for the reading of entire texts, and StudySync® strongly recommends that students seek out and purchase the whole literary or informational work in order to experience it as the author intended. Links to online resellers are available in our digital library. In addition, complete works may be ordered through an authorized reseller by filling out and returning to StudySync® the order form enclosed in this workbook.

Reading & Writing
Companion

113

Skill: Reasons and Relevant Evidence

••• CHECKLIST FOR REASONS AND RELEVANT EVIDENCE

As you begin to determine what reasons and relevant evidence will support your claim(s), use the following questions as a guide:

- What is the claim (or claims) that I am making in my argument?

- What textual evidence am I using to support this claim? Is it relevant?

- Am I quoting the source accurately?

- Does my evidence display logical reasoning and relate to the claim I am making?

Use the following steps as a guide to help you determine how you will support your claim(s) with logical reasoning and relevant evidence, using accurate and credible sources:

- Identify the claim(s) you will make in your argument.

- Select evidence from credible sources that will convince others to accept your claim(s).

  > Look for reliable and relevant sources of information online, such as government or educational websites.

  > Search print resources such as books written by an expert or authority on a topic.

- Explain the connection between your claim(s) and the evidence selected, demonstrating your understanding of the topic or text.

- Think about whether your reasoning is logical and develops naturally from the evidence you have found to support your claim.

↻ YOUR TURN

Reread paragraphs 17–25 of *Refugee* by Alan Gratz. Then, using the checklist on the previous page, answer the multiple-choice questions below.

This question has two parts. First, answer Part A. Then, answer Part B.

Part A: Which of the following best describes a claim the reader can make about this passage?

○ A. Isolation takes away a person's ability to lead a fulfilling life.

○ B. When a group of people is much larger than other groups, that group often exerts control over members of other groups.

○ C. There are no differences between being a superhero in a comic book and being a superhero in reality.

○ D. When a government commits violence against groups of people, it can encourage civilians to commit violence against each other as well.

Part B: Which textual evidence most strongly supports the claim from Part A?

○ A. "Khalid was a Shia Muslim in a country of mostly Sunni Muslims."

○ B. "The differences between Sunnis and Shiites was an excuse. These boys had just wanted to beat someone up."

○ C. "With a battle cry that would have made Wolverine proud, Mahmoud had launched himself at Khalid's attackers."

○ D. "That's when Mahmoud had realized that together, he and Khalid were bigger targets; alone, it was easier to be invisible."

YOUR TURN

Complete the chart by writing a piece of textual evidence from each selection you've chosen that strongly supports your claim, or thesis statement.

My Presentation	Thesis and Textual Evidence
Thesis Statement:	
Selection #1:	
Selection #2:	
Selection #3:	

Skill:
Sources and Citations

••• CHECKLIST FOR SOURCES AND CITATIONS

In order to cite and gather relevant information from multiple print and digital sources, do the following:

- Select and gather information from a variety of print and digital sources using search terms effectively to narrow your search.

- Check that sources are credible and accurate.

- Quote or paraphrase the data you find and cite it to avoid plagiarism, using parenthetical citations, footnotes, or endnotes to credit sources.

- Be sure that facts, details, and other information support the central idea or claim.

- Include all sources in a bibliography, following a standard format:

  > Halall, Ahmed. *The Pyramids of Ancient Egypt.* New York: Central Publishing, 2016.

  > For a citation, footnote, or endnote, include the author, title, and page number.

To check that sources are gathered and cited correctly, consider the following questions:

- Did I quote or paraphrase the data I found and cite it to avoid plagiarism?

- Have I relied on one source, instead of looking for different points of view on my topic in other sources?

- Did I include all my sources in my bibliography or works cited?

- Are my citations formatted correctly using a standard, accepted format?

Please note that excerpts and passages in the StudySync® library and this workbook are intended as touchstones to generate interest in an author's work. The excerpts and passages do not substitute for the reading of entire texts, and StudySync® strongly recommends that students seek out and purchase the whole literary or informational work in order to experience it as the author intended. Links to online resellers are available in our digital library. In addition, complete works may be ordered through an authorized reseller by filling out and returning to StudySync® the order form enclosed in this workbook.

Reading & Writing Companion   **117**

YOUR TURN

Read each of the scenarios below. Then, complete the chart by sorting the scenarios into those that need to be cited and those that do not.

Scenarios	
A	Kristen includes a video she found on a news website in her presentation.
B	Kristen uses her own words to explain why she no longer wants to compete in horseback riding.
C	Kristen mentions the date when Churchill became prime minister in her presentation, and she sees that this date is a fact in many different sources.
D	Kristen quotes an expert from an outside source, either a book or a reliable website.

Needs to Be Cited	Does Not Need to Be Cited

✏ **WRITE**

Use the questions in the checklist section to revise your works cited list. Check that your information, whether quoted or paraphrased, is properly cited to avoid plagiarism. Refer to the *MLA Handbook* as needed.

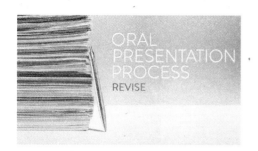

Oral Presentation Process: Revise

PLAN	DRAFT	REVISE	EDIT AND PRESENT

You have written a draft of your oral presentation. You have also received input from your peers about how to improve it. Now you are going to revise your draft.

◀◀ REVISION GUIDE

Examine your draft to find areas for revision. Keep in mind your purpose and audience as you revise for clarity, development, organization, and style. Use the guide below to help you review:

Review	Revise	Example
Clarity		
Identify areas in which multimedia or visual displays can clarify the information that you present.	Focus on one area that needs to be clarified and plan how to clarify that information by integrating multimedia and/or visual displays.	With Wiesel's speech in mind, we can turn to *The Diary of Anne Frank*.  This is a photo of Anne Frank writing in 1940. It was taken before she went into hiding and before the Nazis sent her family to a concentration camp.

Review	Revise	Example
Development		
Identify ideas in your presentation that are not developed with evidence and reasons. Annotate places where your argument lacks support.	Focus on a single claim and add details that help explain your ideas.	In a historic speech, Churchill ~~said that the war was about to become more difficult.~~ announced that this war would involve "many long months of struggle and suffering."
Organization		
Reread your draft and annotate any points that do not logically follow from the other points that you have made.	Focus on one of the points that you identified. If it is relevant, revise some of the sentences in your draft. They should clearly show how this point adds to your argument. If it is not relevant, move the point to a separate section of the presentation.	**Review:** Churchill, Wiesel, and Frank all chose to tell the truth in moments of extreme crisis, and their actions show us how to act in our everyday lives. ~~Even though some facts can be difficult to learn, they help others deepen or change their understanding of a conflict.~~
Style: Word Choice		
Identify sentences with repetitive word choice. Annotate places where you could substitute synonyms and similar phrases for the repetitive wording.	Rewrite sentences with repetitive language by using synonyms or phrases that have a similar meaning.	What should you do when the truth seems too painful to tell? I knew I had to ~~tell my mother the truth~~ be honest with my mother, and some selections that we read helped me understand why. Winston Churchill, Elie Wiesel, and Anne Frank are examples of people who had the courage to share difficult truths in much more trying situations.

Review	Revise	Example
Style: Sentence Variety		
Look for series of sentences that have similar lengths. Annotate any places where a conjunction or transition could vary the length of sentences you use.	Shorten a section of long sentences or join shorter sentences together.	In May of 1940, Churchill was elected as prime minister of the United Kingdom. ~~, but this was not a moment to celebrate.~~ ~~because the.~~ The United Kingdom was at war, and Churchill needed to address a devastating defeat. ~~even~~ Even though it could not have been easy, Churchill was honest about the situation.

✏️ WRITE

Use the guide above, as well as your peer reviews, to help you evaluate your oral presentation to determine areas that should be revised.

Grammar: Writing for Effect

Verb Voice

Rule	Example
A verb in the active voice shows that the subject of the sentence is performing the action in that sentence.	All day, Phineas must keep an eye on his drillers to make sure they stay ahead. All day, Phineas must keep an eye on his diggers to make sure they keep up. Phineas Gage: A Gruesome but True Story About Brain Science
A verb in the passive voice shows that the subject of the sentence is not performing the action in that sentence. It may emphasize the action in a sentence or show that the actor, or "doer," of that action is unknown.	Those skills weren't passed down and the tradition was lost. The Vanishing Island

Verb Mood

Rule	Example
The conditional mood indicates an action that is based on a possible condition. In other words, the condition could have happened, could be true now, or could happen in the future.	But if you do like what I have to offer, you make me an offer I can't refuse. Deal? Teen Mogul
The subjunctive mood indicates an action that is based on an imaginary condition. In other words, that condition is not possible or is contrary to fact.	If they were only where they could buy I should be so loaded with baggage, I should never be able to get home. Letters of a Civil War Nurse
The subjunctive mood also expresses a wish or suggestion.	"I wish the reporters were here," he said at last. Ten Days in a Mad-House

↻ YOUR TURN

1. A writer is sharing an example of Newton's first law of motion. He wants to emphasize that the condition in this statement can happen. In addition, he wants to emphasize the actor in this sentence. How can he revise the sentence below to achieve that effect?

> If Mark applies a force to an object, then the velocity of that object were to change.

- ○ A. If Mark had applied a force to an object, then the velocity of that object had changed.
- ○ B. If Mark were to apply a force to an object, then the velocity of that object would change.
- ○ C. If a force were applied by Mark to an object, then the velocity of that object will change.
- ○ D. If Mark applies a force to an object, then the velocity of that object will change.

2. One writer is a researcher in Hawaii, but she is imagining life as a researcher in Antarctica today. How can she revise the sentence below to show that her statement is imaginary?

> If I was a researcher in Antarctica today, I study glaciers.

- ○ A. If I am a researcher in Antarctica today, I will study glaciers.
- ○ B. If I were a researcher in Antarctica today, I would study glaciers.
- ○ C. If I were a researcher in Antarctica today, I will study glaciers.
- ○ D. If I am a researcher in Antarctica today, I would study glaciers.

3. Which of the following voices or moods is **best** showcased in the following sentence?

> I suggest that Riley become the magazine editor.

- ○ A. Active voice
- ○ B. Passive voice
- ○ C. Conditional mood
- ○ D. Subjunctive mood

Please note that excerpts and passages in the StudySync® library and this workbook are intended as touchstones to generate interest in an author's work. The excerpts and passages do not substitute for the reading of entire texts, and StudySync® strongly recommends that students seek out and purchase the whole literary or informational work in order to experience it as the author intended. Links to online resellers are available in our digital library. In addition, complete works may be ordered through an authorized reseller by filling out and returning to StudySync® the order form enclosed in this workbook.

Reading & Writing
Companion

123

Grammar:
Participial Phrases

Participial Phrases

A participle is a verb form, or verbal, that functions as an adjective. A participial phrase begins with a present or past participle and includes other words that complete its meaning. The entire phrase functions as an adjective. Be sure to place the phrase as close as possible to the modified word in order to make the meaning of the sentence clear.

Correct	Incorrect
Urged on by its fans, the basketball team began its comeback.	The basketball team began its comeback urged on by its fans.
Tammy, **throwing the water balloon**, aimed at the target.	Tammy aimed at the target throwing the water balloon.

Follow these punctuation rules when using participial phrases:

Rule	Text
Use a comma to set off a participial phrase that begins a sentence.	**Preoccupied by the thought of going into hiding**, I stuck the craziest things in the bag, but I'm not sorry. Anne Frank: The Diary of a Young Girl
Use commas to set off a participial phrase that is not essential to the meaning of the sentence.	Upon my arrival to the Poston Relocation Center, I stood bewildered, **glaring at the hot dusty desert, wondering how we could survive.** Dear Miss Breed
No punctuation is necessary when the phrase is not at the beginning of the sentence and is essential to the meaning of the sentence.	A house **divided against itself** cannot stand. House Divided Speech

Copyright © BookheadEd Learning, LLC

YOUR TURN

1. How should this sentence be changed?

> Tapping her way up Pearl Street Margie was the hit of the parade.

○ A. Insert a comma after the word **up**.
○ B. Insert a comma after the word **Street**.
○ C. Insert commas after the word **Street** and after the word **hit**.
○ D. No change needs to be made to this sentence.

2. How should this sentence be changed?

> The dog, lapping up water so fast, must have been very thirsty.

○ A. Delete the comma after **dog**.
○ B. Delete the comma after **fast**.
○ C. Delete the commas after the word **dog** and after the word **fast**.
○ D. No change needs to be made to this sentence.

3. How should this sentence be changed?

> Jason, working, on a shrimp boat enjoyed his summer.

○ A. Delete the commas after the word **Jason** and after the word **working**.
○ B. Delete the comma after the word **working** and insert a comma after the word **boat**.
○ C. Delete the comma after the word **Jason** and insert a comma after the word **boat**.
○ D. No change needs to be made to this sentence.

4. How should this sentence be changed?

> The tall man wearing the gray suit is the judge.

○ A. Insert a comma after the word **man**.
○ B. Insert a comma after the word **suit**.
○ C. Insert commas after the word **man** and after the word **suit**.
○ D. No change needs to be made to this sentence.

Please note that excerpts and passages in the StudySync® library and this workbook are intended as touchstones to generate interest in an author's work. The excerpts and passages do not substitute for the reading of entire texts, and StudySync® strongly recommends that students seek out and purchase the whole literary or informational work in order to experience it as the author intended. Links to online resellers are available in our digital library. In addition, complete works may be ordered through an authorized reseller by filling out and returning to StudySync® the order form enclosed in this workbook.

Reading & Writing Companion   125

Grammar: Gerunds and Gerund Phrases

A gerund is a verb form that ends in *-ing* and acts as a noun. A gerund phrase includes the gerund and all the other words that complete its meaning. A gerund phrase is used as a noun phrase in a sentence. That means that a gerund phrase can be the subject of the sentence, the direct object of a verb, and the object of a preposition.

Text	Explanation
Coming first didn't matter if you couldn't study at all. I Am Malala	The gerund phrase *coming first* is the subject of this sentence.
. . . and he disliked **asking for work**. Born Worker	The gerund phrase *asking for work* is the direct object of the verb *disliked*.
Its purpose is to keep you from **touching this world of the past** in any way. A Sound of Thunder	The gerund phrase *touching this world of the past* is the object of the preposition *from*.

⟳ YOUR TURN

1. Decide if the bold phrase is a gerund phrase used as a subject, direct object, or object of a preposition, or not a gerund phrase at all.

> **Taking dance lessons** was a very good idea.

○ A. subject
○ B. direct object
○ C. object of the preposition
○ D. not a gerund phrase

2. Decide if the bold phrase is a gerund phrase used as a subject, direct object, or object of a preposition, or not a gerund phrase at all.

> Have you ever heard of **dancing a jig** to the songs that whales make?

○ A. subject
○ B. direct object
○ C. object of the preposition
○ D. not a gerund phrase

3. Decide if the bold phrase is a gerund phrase used as a subject, direct object, or object of a preposition, or not a gerund phrase at all.

> **Using her fingers** to knead dough helps with Connie's arthritis.

○ A. subject
○ B. direct object
○ C. object of the preposition
○ D. not a gerund phrase

4. Decide if the bold phrase is a gerund phrase used as a subject, direct object, or object of a preposition, or not a gerund phrase at all.

> Keep your earphones handy for **hearing the latest news**.

○ A. subject
○ B. direct object
○ C. object of the preposition
○ D. not a gerund phrase

Grammar: Run-On Sentences

A run-on sentence is two or more sentences incorrectly written as one sentence. Run-on sentences can confuse readers; correcting them adds variety to the writing, clarifies ideas, and keeps readers interested. Correct a run-on sentence by doing one of the following:

- Change the independent clauses into two separate sentences with a period.
- Separate the independent clauses with a semicolon (;).
- Separate the independent clauses with a comma and a coordinating conjunction (*and*, *or*, *but*).
- Separate the independent clauses with a subordinating conjunction (*because*, *although*, etc.) to create a complex sentence.

Be sure to check that the subject and verb in each clause agree in number.

Run-on Sentence	Correction	Example
Death carries mothers and uncles off to the other world their children and violins remain upon the earth.	Add a subordinating conjunction.	Death carries mothers and uncles off to the other world, **while** their children and violins remain upon the earth. Home
This, however, did not vex me it would not be heard through the wall.	Add a semicolon.	This, however, did not vex me; it would not be heard through the wall. The Tell-Tale Heart

↻ YOUR TURN

1. How should this sentence be changed?

> I went there last year I canceled my reservation this year.

- ○ A. Add a comma after **year**.
- ○ B. Add *because* after **year**.
- ○ C. Add a comma and *but* after the word **year**.
- ○ D. No change needs to be made to this sentence.

2. How should this sentence be changed?

> Some students do their homework after school others do their homework in study hall.

- ○ A. Add a comma after **students** and after the word **school**.
- ○ B. Add a comma after **school**.
- ○ C. Add *while* after the word **school**.
- ○ D. No change needs to be made to this sentence.

3. How should this sentence be changed?

> Air is taken into the lungs oxygen is absorbed into the bloodstream.

- ○ A. Add a semicolon after **lungs**.
- ○ B. Add a semicolon and the coordinating conjunction *but* before **oxygen**.
- ○ C. Add a comma after **lungs**.
- ○ D. No change needs to be made in this sentence.

4. How should this sentence be changed?

> The game was close, but we won it in the last minute.

- ○ A. Delete the comma.
- ○ B. Replace **but** with *so*.
- ○ C. Replace the comma with a semicolon.
- ○ D. No change needs to be made to this sentence.

Please note that excerpts and passages in the StudySync® library and this workbook are intended as touchstones to generate interest in an author's work. The excerpts and passages do not substitute for the reading of entire texts, and StudySync® strongly recommends that students seek out and purchase the whole literary or informational work in order to experience it as the author intended. Links to online resellers are available in our digital library. In addition, complete works may be ordered through an authorized reseller by filling out and returning to StudySync® the order form enclosed in this workbook.

Reading & Writing Companion   129

Oral Presentation Process:
Edit and Present

PLAN	DRAFT	REVISE	EDIT AND PRESENT

You have revised your argumentative oral presentation based on your peer feedback and your own examination.

Now, it is time to edit your oral presentation. When you revised, you focused on the content of your presentation. You probably looked at your presentation's clarity, development, and organization. When you edit, you focus on the mechanics of your oral presentation, paying close attention to things like grammar and punctuation.

Use the checklist below to guide you as you edit:

☐ Have I used gerund phrases correctly?

☐ Have I used participial phrases correctly?

☐ Have I used verb voice and verb mood to create different effects?

☐ Do I have any sentence fragments or run-on sentences?

☐ Have I spelled everything correctly?

Notice some edits Kristen has made:

• Corrected a sentence fragment and run-on sentence.

• Corrected a gerund phrase that is used as the object of a preposition.

• Replaced the passive voice with the active voice to emphasize the "doer" of an action.

• Corrected spelling errors.

Evidence and Analysis #3: Her father, Otto Frank, was the only person in her family who survived the Holocaust. ~~Editing and publishing~~ He edited and published her diaries as a way to make her writing live on after her death.

Evidence and Analysis #3 (Continued): In Anne's diary, she describes hopes, interests, and ~~conflicts that sound so familure~~ conflicts. For example, she tries to make her space in the annex ~~seam~~ seem happier by ~~decorate~~ decorating it with postcards and pictures of movie stars. At the same time, Frank ~~is constantly faced with~~ constantly faces the possibility of being found by the Nazis. That information was hard for me to read, but she was sharing facts and details that we need to know. Her words remind me that millions of people had their lives cut short by hatred and war. To make sure that does not happen again, I must ~~avocate~~ advocate for people in need and share truths that are not easy to hear.

✏ WRITE

Use the questions on the previous page, as well as your peer reviews, to help you evaluate your oral presentation to determine areas that need editing. Then edit your oral presentation to correct those errors.

Once you have made all your corrections, you are ready to present your work. You can distribute your writing to family and friends, hang it on a bulletin board, or post it on your blog. If you publish online, share the link with your family, friends, and classmates.

The Blitz

INFORMATIONAL TEXT

Introduction

In September 1940, the Germans had already taken great steps toward winning World War II. They had defeated many of their enemies, but Great Britain remained a threat. In an attempt to defeat the British Air Force once and for all, Adolf Hitler and his military leaders decided to launch a devastating aerial attack on England. This attack was called the Blitz. It caused catastrophic damage to British property, but it did not break British spirits.

V VOCABULARY

enemy
a person or group that fights against another person or group

determination
the ability to keep trying to achieve a difficult goal

invade
to enter into an area to take control of it

munition
military supplies, including weapons

resilient
able to recover from damage or stress

≡ READ

 NOTES

1   In World War II, Great Britain and Germany were **enemies**. In September 1940, German airplanes began to bomb Britain. The bombing lasted for eight months. More than 40,000 British people were killed. The bombing was called the Blitz. *Blitz* comes from the German word *blitzkrieg*, which means "lightning attack."

Example of WWII era bomber planes

2   Germany had already defeated almost all of the countries in Western Europe. Great Britain was the only large country in the area still fighting Germany. German leader Adolf Hitler wanted to knock out the British air force. This would make it easier for the German army to **invade** Britain. The Germans thought victory would be a piece of cake, but they were wrong.

3   Edward R. Murrow, a U.S. reporter near London, said, "The fires up the river had turned the moon blood red." One business owner told him that the bombing terrified the animals in London.

4   The Germans liked to attack at night, making it harder for British pilots to defend themselves. The pilots' wives never could be sure that their husbands would return. In addition, British soldiers needed searchlights. Some of their guns were positioned along cliffs in coastal areas.

5   Hitler expected that months of bombing would cause the British to be at their wit's end, but they remained **resilient**. British prime minister Winston Churchill encouraged people to be brave. The king and queen of England refused to leave London.

6   The British people showed **determination**. Citizens turned themselves into a defense force to help their military. These heroes helped their cities after the attacks. Their jobs included fighting fires and driving ambulances.

7   The Germans focused on parts of Britain with many people and **munitions** factories. On November 14, 1940, the Germans dropped 500 tons of bombs on Coventry. These bombs included incendiary bombs, which caused fires and terrible destruction. Residents of the city immediately began to rebuild neighborhoods.

Coventry, England, was bombed by German soldiers in November 1940. © IWM (H 5603)

8   In London, people slept underground in the subway tunnels. Some even lived there. British cities suffered serious damage. Still, the British kept fighting. The Germans were not able to weaken their **enemy** enough to invade the country.

9   The Blitz finally ended in May 1941, when Germany decided to attack the Soviet Union and needed its planes for that battle. The British people could finally breathe a sigh of relief.

Adapting to life in the UK. Two women stand amid leveled ruins.
Courtesy of The U.S. National Archives and Records Administration
photo no. 111-SC-178801

10 Later, the British gave the Germans a taste of their own medicine when they bombed German cities continually. When all was said and done, the British air force had the last laugh.

Please note that excerpts and passages in the StudySync® library and this workbook are intended as touchstones to generate interest in an author's work. The excerpts and passages do not substitute for the reading of entire texts, and StudySync® strongly recommends that students seek out and purchase the whole literary or informational work in order to experience it as the author intended. Links to online resellers are available in our digital library. In addition, complete works may be ordered through an authorized reseller by filling out and returning to StudySync® the order form enclosed in this workbook.

Reading & Writing Companion   135

THE BLITZ

First Read

Read the text. After you read, answer the Think Questions below.

☁ THINK QUESTIONS

1. Why did Germany bomb Great Britain?

   _____

   _____

2. At what time did the Germans like to drop their bombs?

   _____

   _____

3. What were some of the jobs of the British defense force?

   _____

   _____

4. Use context to confirm the meaning of the word *resilient* as it is used in "The Blitz." Write your definition of *resilient* here.

   _____

   _____

5. What is another way to say that a person is *determined*?

   _____

   _____

Skill:
Analyzing Expressions

★ DEFINE

When you read, you may find English expressions that you do not know. An **expression** is a group of words that communicates an idea. Two types of expressions are **idioms** and **sayings**. They can be difficult to understand because the meanings of the words are different from their **literal**, or usual, meanings.

An **idiom** is an expression that is commonly known among a group of people. For example: "It's raining cats and dogs" means it is raining heavily. **Sayings** are short expressions that contain advice or wisdom. For instance: "Don't count your chickens before they hatch" means do not plan on something good happening before it happens. Neither expression is about actual animals.

••• CHECKLIST FOR ANALYZING EXPRESSIONS

✓ If you find a confusing group of words, it may be an expression. The meaning of words in expressions may not be their literal meaning.

• Ask yourself: Is this confusing because the words are new? Or because the words do not make sense together?

✓ Determining the overall meaning may require that you use one or more of the following:

• context clues

• a dictionary or other resource

• teacher or peer support

✓ Highlight important information before and after the expression to look for clues.

Please note that excerpts and passages in the StudySync® library and this workbook are intended as touchstones to generate interest in an author's work. The excerpts and passages do not substitute for the reading of entire texts, and StudySync® strongly recommends that students seek out and purchase the whole literary or informational work in order to experience it as the author intended. Links to online resellers are available in our digital library. In addition, complete works may be ordered through an authorized reseller by filling out and returning to StudySync® the order form enclosed in this workbook.

Reading & Writing Companion 137

YOUR TURN

Read the following excerpt from the text. Then, complete the multiple-choice questions below.

---

from "The Blitz"

The Germans liked to attack at night, making it harder for British pilots to defend themselves. The pilots' wives never could be sure that their husbands would return. In addition, British soldiers needed searchlights. Some of their guns were positioned along cliffs in coastal areas.

Hitler expected that months of bombing would cause the British to be at their wit's end, but they remained resilient. British prime minister Winston Churchill encouraged people to be brave. The king and queen of England refused to leave London.

---

1. What does "at their wit's end" mean in this text?

   ○ A. to be very brave
   ○ B. to refuse to leave
   ○ C. to be very upset
   ○ D. to come to an end

2. Which context clue helped you determine the meaning of the expression?

   ○ A. "The pilots' wives never could be sure . . ."
   ○ B. ". . . British soldiers needed searchlights."
   ○ C. "Hitler expected that months of bombing . . ."
   ○ D. ". . . but they remained resilient."

Skill:
Visual and Contextual Support

★ DEFINE

Visual support is an image or an object that helps you understand a text. **Contextual support** is a **feature** that helps you understand a text. By using visual and contextual supports, you can develop your vocabulary so you can better understand a variety of texts.

First, preview the text to identify any visual supports. These might include illustrations, graphics, charts, or other objects in a text. Then, identify any contextual supports. Examples of contextual supports are titles, heads, captions, and boldface terms. Write down your **observations**.

Then, write down what those visual and contextual supports tell you about the meaning of the text. Note any new vocabulary that you see in those supports. Ask your peers and your teacher to confirm your understanding of the text.

••• CHECKLIST FOR VISUAL AND CONTEXTUAL SUPPORT

To use visual and contextual support to understand texts, do the following:

- ✓ Preview the text. Read the title, headers, and other features. Look at any images and graphics.

- ✓ Write down the visual and contextual supports in the text.

- ✓ Write down what those supports tell you about the text.

- ✓ Note any new vocabulary that you see in those supports.

- ✓ Confirm your observations with your peers and teacher.

- ✓ Create an illustration for the reading and write a descriptive caption.

↻ YOUR TURN

Read the following excerpt from the text. Then, complete the multiple-choice questions below.

---

from "The Blitz"

The Germans focused on parts of Britain with many people and munitions factories. On November 14, 1940, the Germans dropped 500 tons of bombs on Coventry. These bombs included incendiary bombs, which caused fires and terrible destruction. Residents of the city immediately began to rebuild neighborhoods.

Coventry, England, was bombed by German soldiers in
November 1940. © IWM (H 5603)

In London, people slept underground in the subway tunnels. Some even lived there. British cities suffered serious damage. Still, the British kept fighting. The Germans were not able to weaken their enemy enough to invade the country.

---

1. The paragraphs in this section are mostly about

   ○ A. the types of factories that the British used.
   ○ B. the neighborhoods where British people lived.
   ○ C. the damage that the bombs caused in England.
   ○ D. the subway tunnels in London.

2. The visual support helps readers to

   ○ A. understand technical terminology.
   ○ B. imagine what the damage looked like.
   ○ C. see the inside of a British factory.
   ○ D. locate the city of Coventry on a map.

THE BLITZ

Close Read

✏ WRITE

INFORMATIVE: The Blitz changed the lives of many people living in England during World War II. Write a paragraph explaining some of the ways that their lives were affected. Be sure to use ideas and details from the text and images. Pay attention to correctly spelling plurals as you write.

Use the checklist below to guide you as you write.

☐ How did the Blitz change the way the British felt?

☐ How did the Blitz change what the British did?

☐ How did the Blitz change the way the British lived?

Use the sentence frames to organize and write your informational paragraph.

The Blitz made the British feel _____.

They felt this way because _____.

During the Blitz, some British citizens decided to _____

_____.

This helped them _____

_____.

After the Blitz, British citizens _____

_____.

They wanted to _____

_____.

Please note that excerpts and passages in the StudySync® library and this workbook are intended as touchstones to generate interest in an author's work. The excerpts and passages do not substitute for the reading of entire texts, and StudySync® strongly recommends that students seek out and purchase the whole literary or informational work in order to experience it as the author intended. Links to online resellers are available in our digital library. In addition, complete works may be ordered through an authorized reseller by filling out and returning to StudySync® the order form enclosed in this workbook.

Reading & Writing Companion 141

A Letter from Robert

DRAMA

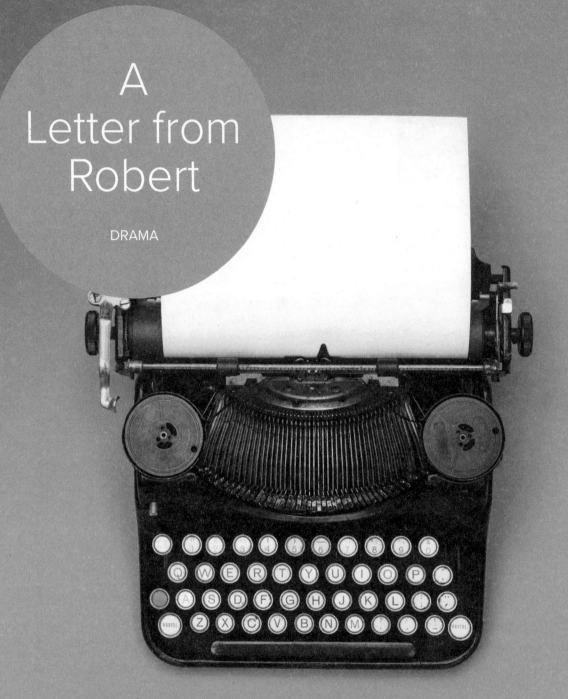

Introduction

This short play takes place in London after the Blitz, a period of intense bombing by the German Air Force during World War II. The Blitz, which lasted eight months from September 1940 to May 1941, destroyed or damaged over one million homes and killed more than 40,000 civilians. In the drama, a grieving mother returns to London after the bombing has ended, only to find that her home has been destroyed.

V VOCABULARY

residential
relating to where people live

dreadful
very bad

debris
pieces left over when an object is destroyed

defense
the act of protecting against an attack

startle
to surprise or scare

≡ READ

NOTES

1   [*A **residential** street in London. July 1941. **Debris** lies between two damaged buildings. MARGARET takes cautious steps. When she reaches the spot that used to be her doorstep, she weeps. The front door of one of the buildings swings open. HELEN steps out.*]

2   HELEN: I was starting to think I'd never see you again!

3   MARGARET (*wiping away tears*): You **startled** me. I'm relieved to see you've survived. Attacking military bases during a war is one thing. But bombing innocent civilians? I had to go. I promised Robert I'd stay safe … You should have come to my sister's.

4   HELEN: It will take more than incendiary bombs to scare me. Broken windows and a hole in the wall. Nothing that can't be fixed. You have my sympathy about your house. You can stay with me until this **dreadful** war ends. No sense in starting construction now.

5 MARGARET (*sadly*): I am leaving London.

6 HELEN (*with surprise*): You can't leave! Who will your son come home to after the war if you're not here?

7 MARGARET: My son won't be coming home. I received a telegram from the Royal Air Force. Robert was killed in combat.

8 HELEN: Stay with me. We will get through this together.

9 MARGARET: There are too many memories. Everywhere there's something that reminds me ... I'll always wish to see him coming around the corner. There is nothing left for me here.

10 HELEN: Some of your things survived the blast. [HELEN *pulls a letter out of her pocket.*]

11 MARGARET: It's Robert's letter. [*begins to read*] "The twenty-second of May, nineteen forty. My dearest mother, two days ago our Prime Minister gave a radio address urging us to ready ourselves for **defense** during these terrible times. These past two days I have thought of little else."

12 [*As MARGARET reads, another voice joins hers, as if coming from a ghost. It is ROBERT'S VOICE.*]

13 MARGARET and ROBERT: "I have thought about the German attacks in France, Denmark, Norway, Belgium, and the Netherlands. As much as it pains me to leave, I know their pain is greater."

14 [MARGARET'S VOICE *dies out, and* ROBERT'S VOICE *continues alone.*]

15 ROBERT'S VOICE: It is my duty to rise up and fight against the forces of evil that are spreading across the continent. I will take my place in the Royal Air Force. I will fight for Britain, for Europe, and, most of all, for you.

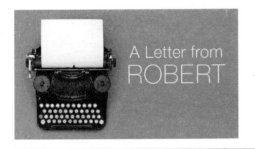

A Letter from
ROBERT

First Read

Read the story. After you read, answer the Think Questions below.

1. What can you infer happened to Margaret's home?

_____

_____

2. Why does Margaret want to move away from London?

_____

_____

3. Why did Robert join the Royal Air Force?

_____

_____

4. Use context to confirm the meaning of the word *debris* as it is used in "A Letter from Robert." Write your definition of *debris* here.

_____

_____

5. The word *defense* contains the Latin prefix *de-*, meaning "away from," and the Latin root *fens*, meaning "strike." Use that information and context clues to guess the meaning of the word *defense* as it is used in "A Letter from Robert." Write your definition of *defense* here.

_____

_____

Please note that excerpts and passages in the StudySync® library and this workbook are intended as touchstones to generate interest in an author's work. The excerpts and passages do not substitute for the reading of entire texts, and StudySync® strongly recommends that students seek out and purchase the whole literary or informational work in order to experience it as the author intended. Links to online resellers are available in our digital library. In addition, complete works may be ordered through an authorized reseller by filling out and returning to StudySync® the order form enclosed in this workbook.

Reading & Writing
Companion

145

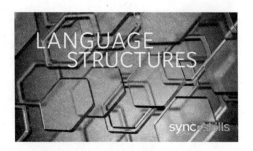

Skill:
Language Structures

 DEFINE

In every language, there are rules that tell how to **structure** sentences. These rules define the correct order of words. In the English language, for example, a **basic** structure for sentences is subject, verb, and object. Some sentences have more **complicated** structures.

You will encounter both basic and complicated **language structures** in the classroom materials you read. Being familiar with language structures will help you better understand the text.

••• CHECKLIST FOR LANGUAGE STRUCTURES

To improve your comprehension of language structures, do the following:

✓ Monitor your understanding.

- Ask yourself: Why do I not understand this sentence? Is it because I do not understand some of the words? Or is it because I do not understand the way the words are ordered in the sentence?

✓ Pay attention to verbs followed by prepositions.

- A **verb** names an action.

    > Example: I **sit** on my chair.

    > This tells the reader what the subject of the sentence is doing (sitting).

- A **preposition** defines the relationship between two or more nouns or verbs in a sentence.

    > Example: I sit **on** my chair.

    > This tells the reader where the subject is doing the action (on a chair).

- Sometimes the preposition comes directly after the verb, but it can also be separated by another word.

  > Example: I **took** it **to** school with me.

- Sometimes the preposition changes the meaning of the verb. This is called a **phrasal verb**.

  > Example: The teacher liked to **call on** the students in the front of the class.

  > The phrasal verb *call on* means "to select someone to share information."

✓ Break down the sentence into its parts.

- Ask yourself: What words make up the verbs in this sentence? Is the verb followed by a preposition? How does this affect the meaning of the sentence?

Please note that excerpts and passages in the StudySync® library and this workbook are intended as touchstones to generate interest in an author's work. The excerpts and passages do not substitute for the reading of entire texts, and StudySync® strongly recommends that students seek out and purchase the whole literary or informational work in order to experience it as the author intended. Links to online resellers are available in our digital library. In addition, complete works may be ordered through an authorized reseller by filling out and returning to StudySync® the order form enclosed in this workbook.

Reading & Writing Companion   **147**

YOUR TURN

Read the following excerpt from paragraphs 1 and 2 of the story. Then, complete the multiple choice questions below.

---

from "A Letter from Robert"

[A residential street in London. July 1941. Debris lies between two damaged buildings. MARGARET takes cautious steps. When she reaches the spot that used to be her doorstep, she weeps. The front door of one of the buildings swings open. HELEN steps out.]

HELEN: I was starting to think I'd never see you again!

---

1. In the second sentence of paragraph 1, the preposition **between** tells about:

    ○ A. who the characters are.

    ○ B. where the debris lies.

    ○ C. what Margaret's house is like.

    ○ D. what Britain and its enemy do.

2. In the fourth sentence of paragraph 1, you can infer that the phrase **used to be** means the same as:

    ○ A. was

    ○ B. is

    ○ C. used up

    ○ D. used by

3. In the last sentence of paragraph 1, what information does the preposition **out** mainly give about the verb **steps**?

    ○ A. what

    ○ B. when

    ○ C. why

    ○ D. where

Skill:
Visual and Contextual Support

★ DEFINE

Visual support is an image or an object that helps you understand a text. **Contextual support** is a **feature** that helps you understand a text. By using visual and contextual supports, you can develop your vocabulary so you can better understand a variety of texts.

First, preview the text to identify any visual supports. These might include illustrations, graphics, charts, or other objects in a text. Then, identify any contextual supports. Examples of contextual supports are titles, heads, captions, and boldface terms. Write down your **observations**.

Then, write down what those visual and contextual supports tell you about the meaning of the text. Note any new vocabulary that you see in those supports. Ask your peers and your teacher to confirm your understanding of the text.

••• CHECKLIST FOR VISUAL AND CONTEXTUAL SUPPORT

To use visual and contextual support to understand texts, do the following:

- ✓ Preview the text. Read the title, headers, and other features. Look at any images and graphics.

- ✓ Write down the visual and contextual supports in the text.

- ✓ Write down what those supports tell you about the text.

- ✓ Note any new vocabulary that you see in those supports.

- ✓ Confirm your observations with your peers and teacher.

- ✓ Create an illustration for the reading and write a descriptive caption.

YOUR TURN

Read the following excerpt from paragraphs 10 to 13 of the story. Then, complete the multiple choice questions below.

---

from "A Letter from Robert"

HELEN: Some of your things survived the blast. [HELEN *pulls a letter out of her pocket.*]

MARGARET: It's Robert's letter. [*begins to read*] "The twenty-second of May, nineteen forty. My dearest mother, two days ago our Prime Minister gave a radio address urging us to ready ourselves for defense during these terrible times. These past two days I have thought of little else."

[*As* MARGARET *reads, another voice joins hers, as if coming from a ghost. It is* ROBERT'S VOICE.]

MARGARET and ROBERT: "I have thought about the German attacks in France, Denmark, Norway, Belgium, and the Netherlands. As much as it pains me to leave, I know their pain is greater."

---

1. The capital letters in this excerpt show:

   ○ A. important vocabulary words

   ○ B. new headers for each section

   ○ C. the names of the characters speaking

   ○ D. the title of the passage

2. The italicized letters in this excerpt show:

   ○ A. stage directions that give additional details

   ○ B. important times and dates

   ○ C. the names of cities and countries

   ○ D. the words from a radio address

3. These contextual supports help readers understand that:

   ○ A. Robert has returned to his home.

   ○ B. Helen wants to share a letter with Margaret.

   ○ C. Margaret is imagining Robert's voice.

   ○ D. Robert is appearing as a ghost.

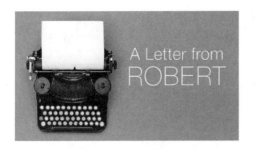

Close Read

✏ WRITE

NARRATIVE: Write a short story based on the drama. Use the same characters and events, but add descriptive details. Make sure to include terms that are appropriate for the time period and setting. Pay attention to possessive case as you write.

Use the checklist below to guide you as you write.

☐ Who are the characters in the play?

☐ What are the main events in the play?

☐ What will happen in your story?

Use the sentence frames to organize and write your short story.

A woman named _____ returned home.

She lived in_____.

She met up with her old neighbor, _____.

Margaret says that she has decided to _____

_____.

She feels _____

because _____.

Helen gives her _____.

PHOTO/IMAGE CREDITS:

studysync

Text Fulfillment Through StudySync

If you are interested in specific titles, please fill out the form below and we will check availability through our partners.

ORDER DETAILS

Date:

TITLE	AUTHOR	Paperback/ Hardcover	Specific Edition *If Applicable*	Quantity

SHIPPING INFORMATION	BILLING INFORMATION ☐ *SAME AS SHIPPING*
Contact:	Contact:
Title:	Title:
School/District:	School/District:
Address Line 1:	Address Line 1:
Address Line 2:	Address Line 2:
Zip or Postal Code:	Zip or Postal Code:
Phone:	Phone:
Mobile:	Mobile:
Email:	Email:

PAYMENT INFORMATION

☐ CREDIT CARD

Name on Card:

Card Number: Expiration Date: Security Code:

☐ PO

Purchase Order Number:

StudySync Text Fulfillment, BookheadEd Learning, LLC
610 Daniel Young Drive | Sonoma, CA 95476